Further Reflections On Churt

Olivia Cotton

Further Reflections on Churt
First published December 2004

Image processing and typesetting by Bruce Bovill

Published by O M Cotton, Court Barn, Churt, Surrey GU10 2NX

ISBN 0-954 2486-1-9

Printed and bound by
Antony Rowe Ltd,
2 Whittle Drive,
Highfield Industrial Estate,
Eastbourne BN23 6QT

Contents

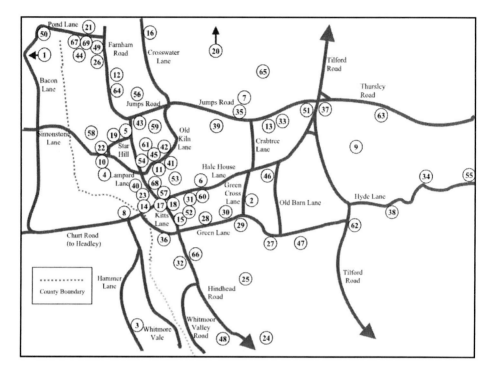

Key to places numbered on the map of Churt

1 Airstrip
2 Anne's Cottage
3 Assisi/Llanover/Follyfield
4 Barford (Court)
5 Beefolds/Threeways
6 Big Oak
7 Borrow House
8 Bridge End
9 Bron-y-de
10 Chinton Hanger
11 Churt Club
12 Churt House
13 Churt Lea/Churt Meadows
14 Churt School & house
15 Court Barn
16 Crosswater Farm
17 Crossways
18 Crossways Pub
19 Edwin Abbott Mem. Cotts
20 Frensham Common
21 Frensham Great Pond
22 Furze Hill
23 Garage
24 Golf Clubhouse

25 Golf Course
26 Gorse Cottage
27 Green Farm
28 Green Lane Cottages
29 Greencroft
30 Greencross Farm
31 Hale House (Farm)
32 Hatch Farm/Road Farm
33 Hopton/Prairie Cottage
34 Hyde Farm
35 Jumps House
36 Kitts Farm
37 LG's Farm Shop
38 Marchants Farm
39 Moorside Cottages
40 Moreton House
41 Old Forge
42 Old Kiln
43 Old Post Office
44 Old Recreation Ground
45 Old Vicarage
46 Outmoor (Farm)
47 Penrhos
48 Pine House

49 Pond Cottage
50 Pond Hotel/White Horse
51 Pride of the Valley Pub
52 Quinnettes
53 Recreation Ground
54 Redhearne Green
55 Ridgeway Farm
56 Sandbrow
57 School Playing Field/Gardens
58 Sidlaws
59 Silverbeck
60 Squirrels
61 St John's Church
62 Stock Farm
63 Stream Cottage
64 The Chase
65 The Devil's Jumps
66 The Hatch
67 Tyndrum
68 Village Hall
69 Woodcote

4

Introduction

By the end of the 19th Century the village of Churt, lying on the border of Surrey and Hampshire, was beginning to come together, albeit loosely. Like most ancient English villages Churt originally comprised scattered habitations whose people, in this case, made a living from the narrow strip of fertile land on an east to west axis.

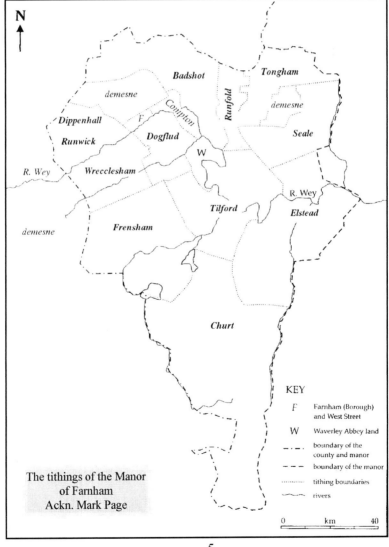

The tithings of the Manor of Farnham
Ackn. Mark Page

The Romans knew Churt as they had a farm at Frensham, on the other side of what is now Frensham Pond though it was then a small natural pond. Later the Saxons left traces of one of their homesteads in Kitts Farm. The King of Wessex in 688, Caedwalla, thought that the land around Churt was a suitable gift to the church as a celebration of his conversion to Christianity. Quickly the gift of land, including Churt, fell into the hands of the Bishop of Winchester so that, some years later, when the Normans conquered Britain, their French-speaking Bishop of Winchester took the land into his Great Manor of Farnham and he became our Lord of the Manor for roughly a thousand years. For more than 300 years, until the English language once again became dominant, French was the tongue of those commanding allegiance from Churt.

Over the centuries that allegiance altered and slackened until finally in 1857 at the "Sale of the Bishop's Waste" (his wasteland, his commons), the ties with the church were broken by the Frensham Enclosure Act and a new style of village life began. Whereas previously all residents had been the Bishop's tenants, following the 1857 Act land then became available for sale and new houses appeared. In Churt these were large houses, with the result that Churt became a village consisting of "Old Families" with their roots in the past and of newcomers in the "Big Houses."

In the latter half of the 19th Century the church and school were built, developments that slowly led to a more cohesive village. Even in 1894 the village did not regard itself as an entity. There were two Churt cricket teams, one based on the recreation ground near the Great Pond, and one based on the area round the Pride of the Valley. The end of each cricket season terminated with a match between the two teams followed by a meal at the inn.

A similar attitude is revealed in 1932 when the vicar noted that, follow-ing the acquisition of a village hall, Churt's village centre had moved from the Jumps Road area to Crossways.

Nowadays Churt has become a unified whole, from Ridgeway Farm to the Pond Hotel, from Pond Lane to the Golf Course. It has a strong community spirit earning it the name of "The Friendly Village." Many of its homes may still be found tucked away in little lanes or on the edge of broad heathlands.

In 2003 Churt became a parish in its own right. Old maps show Churt as one of the thirteen tithings of the Great Manor of Farnham (see page 5), though by the 13th Century it had become a tithing of Frensham parish.

In this book will be found living memories of two nonagenarians, and other elderly residents who have worked or dwelt here and recall the Churt they knew in times past. From archive documents come further details of events and places familiar to us in present-day Churt. All will help to give an idea of the altering lifestyles in our village over the decades.

1: An Old Family: the Crouchers

Our first nonagenarian is a well-known figure in Churt – Ruth Deadman, formerly Croucher. As Ruth reminisces she brings alive an earlier time in our village.

The Crouchers have a long history in Churt. More than seven centuries ago in 1294 William atte Cruce held land situated at the cross roads of Green Lane and Green Cross Lane. Some give another interpretation for 'atte cruce' and consider it to mean land where there was a religious cross; crosses were not uncommon. In time the name evolved to Croucher so that in 1349 Richard atte Croucher is noted in the Pipe Rolls as owing 8 shillings 4 pence in rent. William Croucher's holdings became associated with Green Cross which was then a tiny hamlet consisting of Greencroft, Greencross, Greencross Farm and at least one more house.

Over the Years the Crouchers inter-married with members of the old families in the village so that Ruth's nephew Edward has been able to create a family tree going back to John Croucher who married Mary Shotter in 1696. A Charles Croucher, born about 1790, owned a grocer's shop at Squirrels in Hale House Lane but enjoyed a little smuggling on the side. Smuggling was indulged in by men of good families. It was not considered a disgrace for a country house to get supplies of spirits and wine from smugglers. Charles' independent lifestyle and his escape from the Revenue Officers has led to a tale which has passed into Churt folklore: his daughters watched the officers search his cottage as they sat demurely on the kegs of brandy, their crinolines concealing the contraband.

Ruth's grandfather John lived at Pond Cottage and was responsible for the quinquennial draining of Frensham Great Pond. He was also licensed to sell sand from round the Great Pond. The heavily-laden horses stopped at the drinking trough on Churt village green on their uphill journey to the turnpike road.

Living in Hatch Farm in 1899 was Stephen Croucher (Ruth's great-uncle), bailiff to Mr Prichard of Llanover who was a generous benefactor to the village.

Ruth was the sixth of seven children, four boys and three girls, born to James Croucher and his wife Ellen (Fullick). James was born in 1860, three years after the Frensham Enclosure Act impelled the village into a new, very different, era when large houses were built on what had formerly been the Bishop's land and their owners provided work for numerous Churt residents, as domestic staff, chauffeurs, gardeners, gamekeepers, etc.

Ruth was born in 1908 and looks back on her childhood with contentment. Born at Copse Cottage in Simonstone Lane, she and her family moved to Mead End – now Moorside Cottages - owned by Mr Allen of Churt Lea. He also owned Outmoor which was home to his gardener Bantock, recipient of the Military Medal in the first world war. Mr Allen, a Quaker, held a church service in his home on Sunday afternoons which Ruth attended, being almost obliged to go. The deference of employees to their employers extended to their families.

Ruth's parents:
James Croucher
and Ellen Croucher
(neé Fullick)

Before they went to school each morning the Croucher children took turns to collect the day's supply of drinking water. They walked half a mile to a spring in the woods and returned with the water which was put into a huge crock for drinking and cooking. Rain water sufficed for other uses. A scary job was buying eggs from Outmoor Farm where the farmer's wife was blind and had to tap her way along the walls to the chicken house. In school holidays, once their domestic jobs were done, the children were free to play and enjoy the woods full of wild flowers. Indoors, paraffin lamps were used downstairs and candles upstairs. They had water, wood and a garden and felt themselves well-supplied.

Travelling salesmen brought a selection of clothes to the door, though rummage sales were the usual suppliers. From Farnham came a salesman with bedding. A shop near the Pride of the Valley, run by Miss Novell and Miss Heath, "sold everything". Without refrigerators milk would not keep fresh all day so a second purchase had to be made in the afternoon from Crosswater Farm, where Ruth would watch Mrs Jim Baker churning butter. By leaving a can and a few pence at Col. Smythe's farm at Barford, families were able to purchase cheap, skimmed milk. Ruth remembers the Colonel with his monocle, reading the lessons at church where he had his own family pew.

Ruth's schooling started in 1912. Her snowy white apron over her dress and her button boots represented her uniform. On their way to school in winter the children would often stop at the forge to warm themselves. The ringing sound of the blacksmith's hammer, the rumble of cart wheels on the stony roads, even the note of the bugle from Bordon army camp were typical accompaniments to her early childhood. In the cold winter months co-coa, made by the older pupils, was available for 2 pence a week. Older boys filled the coal scuttles for the open fires but, during the Great War when coal was rationed, the schoolchildren collected wood to keep the school fires burning. There was plenty of wood for the Croucher children to take from the wood opposite their home, where trees were sold for pit props. Even so, at the back of the room it was so cold that children wore gloves and scarves in class. In a National School there was strong emphasis on

Button boots in a painting by
Birket Foster

religious education. Prayers and a hymn started the day. Before school paused for lunch the children sang:

Be present at our table Lord
Be here and everywhere adored
May manna to our souls be given
The bread of life sent down from heaven.

After the meal they sang:

Thank you Lord for this our food
And thank you Lord for all things good.

Each week the vicar took a scripture lesson when pupils were expected to know the catechism, the commandments, the Lord's prayer and one psalm. Each year the diocesan inspector reviewed the children's progress and issued scripture certificates. Ruth gained a certificate on two consecutive years; a third signature on the document would have entitled her to a half holiday. On the death of St John's vicar, Mr Watson, in 1917 each child took a white flower to school to create a wreath.

Attendance Certificate for William Tickner

Daily attendance figures were recorded on an attendance board; it was the duty of the senior boys to add up the various columns and produce an overall figure for the whole school. In March 1895 the authorities announced: "With the hope of encouraging the regular attendance of children the village magazine will publish the names of those who have made every possible attendance". For months afterwards the names of best-attending children appeared in the monthly church magazine.

School was not always idyllic. Ruth's brother Will so disliked his headmaster, Mr Rankine, later a well-known local archaeologist, that on his departure in 1911 for Badshot Lea School Will vowed to give him the thrashing he deserved as soon as he was old enough. The resolve was never carried out.

The first world war at Churt introduced harsh reality to a young child. The memory of a picture of an overturned gun-carriage with its dead horses alongside has remained with Ruth ever since. The prisoners-of-war coming weekly to collect their mail from the post office at Jumps Road were frightening although Ruth was conscious that they looked little and poor. She assumed they were Serbs. Her wartime memories include the laying up of the Canadian colours in St John's Church and, much later, their return to the regiment by Mr Barton, successor to Mr Watson who died in 1917.

Front row, right: Mrs Martin, who ran the Post Office at Jumps Road

Playing with iron hoops, made by the village blacksmith, was a regular pastime. On one occasion Ruth and her brothers heard the sound of a motor car approaching slowly. Eager to see this rarity they mounted one of the many heaps of stone at the side of the unmade-up road to enjoy their first sight of a car. At a crucial moment Ruth let go of her hoop in amazement. It struck the car. The chauffeur stopped and a furious lady-owner dismounted. She reported Ruth to the local policeman but he, knowing Ruth, accepted her word that it was a total accident. Let's hope there was adequate insurance in those days.

The Jumps were a popular spot for games. The Cottrell children, Susan and James, who lived at nearby Borrow House, would show Ruth and friends the tunnel built in the 19th Century under one of the Jumps by the astronomer Carrington whose home was Jumps House. Through the winding tunnel they went until the Cottrells would race away laughing, leaving them to find their own way out. At that time the Jumps were known locally as Tree Jump, Cave Jump and Stoney Jump.

The Devil's Jumps

After leaving school at 14, Ruth's first job was as a dormitory maid at Melbreck School on the Tilford Road, run by the Verneys for small boys. Two years later she joined the living-in staff at the vicarage, Mr Bosanquet having taken over the living in 1925. She worked hard but was happy. The lamps were paraffin, but the vicarage had the luxury of piped water in 1924, though a well still remained in the kitchen. Water was a precious thing in houses and cottages. At a time of great class distinction Ruth had to admit visitors to the vicarage according to their social status – to the church room, the study, or the drawing room. Never had she to be seen at the gate, nor without her cap. When her father was gardener at the vicarage Ruth made a point of smuggling him tea at lunch times.

At the age of 25 Ruth was married from the vicarage to Fred Deadman, a decorator. They lived at Sandy Lane, Rushmoor until Green Lane Cottages were built. Part of Sandy Lane Cottages was known as China Town but why this should be is not known. When World War II broke out her husband volunteered for the airforce and was abroad for most of the hostilities.

Meanwhile Ruth was helping at Greencroft, a home originally converted by Mr West from two old Tudor cottages with the aid of old ship's beams. In the kitchen was the well. At Greencroft she became almost part of the family, as a Nanny, looking after the West children who now, with children of their own, are regular visitors at Ruth's home.

Ruth at 96 is a much-loved member of Churt's community. Alert, interesting and interested, she remains positive, "On the whole change has been for the better. In the old days families were very poor, wages were low. None of nature's bounty was wasted; heath-brooms were made for neighbours; bracken was gathered for mulch; whortleberries and blackberries provided food; silver-sand from the common cleaned and sharpened knives." It was a safe time for children, who had more freedom to roam on the common. There were slate clubs to help in times of emergency. Everyone had a garden and consequently fruit and vegetables. "Nowadays," Ruth mused " there is better education for every child. They were hard days but happy. I am fortunate to be in Churt where the elderly are looked after."

So much of Churt's early 20th Century history is to be learned from Ruth. She explains that her elder sister Ellen, known as Nellie, was a pretty girl and posed as a fisher girl for one of the paintings by Bryan Hook, son of the well-known Victorian painter, James Clark Hook of Silverbeck. So far that particular painting has not been located.

Will Croucher in 1967
(newspaper cutting)

15

Will Croucher, Ruth's older brother, will long be remembered for his "Memoirs", a hand-written account of life in Churt from 1900 until 1965. At a time of tied cottages for workers on farms and big estates, few cottages were generally available so that the 1930s' conversion of these few dwellings into weekend cottages for outsiders aroused Will's bitter condemnation.

Another brother Len Croucher, born 1916, was a respected and successful gardener in the village. At a time when larger houses had 2, 3 or more gardeners, and when entry forms for the annual flower show displayed the gardeners' names, Len's duties at Barford Court included Sunday work on the two tennis courts which had to be mown and marked out ready for the afternoon tennis parties. His army service in World War II with the Queen's Royal West Surrey Regiment included captivity as a prisoner of war. After the war he worked at Court Barn for the Bullock family who later presented Len with a house in Hale House Lane.

Len Croucher in the garden of Court Barn

A further brother, Ernest, left his name to a portion of the village. "Ernie's Corner" is situated at the top of Old Kiln Close and is in the general area where the original 1880s Institute was sited. Though the name, Ernie's Corner, has nowadays almost disappeared, Croucher and Deadman are still familiar names recognised and respected in the village of Churt.

2: Life in the Big Houses

It is difficult to find records relating to the owners of the Big Houses. We are fortunate in having had access to a record of life at Chinton Hanger in the Edwardian period as portrayed in a "Family Chronicle", comprising letters circulating among 23 members of one family. The letters were edited and circulated by Emily Ann Simon and included correspondence from Lady Napier of Chinton Hanger.

A view of the back of Chinton Hanger in 1909

Chinton Hanger

Chinton Hanger was built in 1904 by Col. Smythe of Barford who later built Moreton House, sometime known as Churt Acres. At one period in its existence Chinton Hanger was named Lowood. The Napiers, who had bought Chinton Hanger in 1909 from Capt. Morris, were looking forward to residence in Churt after their life in Singapore.

Details of their early days in Churt come from the "Family Chronicle".a composite newsletter providing information to 23 members of a large family of German origin, among whom was Susie Stoehr, later to become Lady Napier.

The idea of a Chronicle had been put forward by Nell Eckhard, one of Susie's seven sisters. Another sister, Emily Anne, undertook the task of editing the quarterly contribution from each correspondent, getting their handwritten documents typed, and then circulating them to the family. At least three of the Stoehr sisters, originally from Saxe Altenburg, settled in England - Emily

The same view as overleaf, in 1983

Simon, the editor, Nell Eckhard and Susie Napier. Each family was intent upon becoming anglicised and all three families sent sons to fight for England in the Great War.

Susie's first episode to the Chronicle was written on 23rd September 1909 when she and Walter Napier (whom she had married as her second husband in 1891) were on board the SS Marmora having left Aden that morning on their way home from Singapore where Walter had first been a partner in the law firm of Drew, Napier, then, for the final two years, Attorney General. Susie was the first woman driver in Singapore. They had already bought Chinton Hanger with its 16 acres from Capt. Morris who was leaving them some of his servants. They expected alterations and redecoration to the property to take several months. Plans for the education of their son and two daughters were in hand.

The second contribution records that that very day, 13th December 1909, Walter was attending an investiture to arise as Sir Walter.

The two newcomers to Churt took advantage of the lectures which were available and attended a series in Farnham on the Poor Law and particularly enjoyed hearing Mr Sydney Webb. Trying to study workhouses, the pair had looked over two at Farnham and Alton where they were impressed by the kindness and sympathy of the two masters. A later lecture at Oxford by Mr Theodore Roosevelt prompted the remark "He is uglier than his pictures". They even attended a lecture at the Cambridge Liberal Club – "the other side politically."

Susie started a Mothers' Union at her home in 1910 where members had a course of cookery lessons – how a family of five could live on 8 shillings per week. The following year 1911 saw the family watching the coronation of King George V from Parliament Square and, later, viewing the lines of ships at Portsmouth for the naval review.

Walter J Napier in his first car
(Baby Peugeot) at Oxford

A field with its "hideous gravel pit, opposite to Chinton Hanger," was purchased by the Napiers "to keep other people from getting hold of it and putting up suburban villas". This was a field mentioned by W D Croucher in his Memoirs recalling that his father dug gravel there for the Rural District Council. The field was quickly tidied by two agricultural workers earning 3 shillings a day, and is where Chinton Cottage now stands.

A court attendance is described in June 1912 when the family had seats in the throne room, an excellent supper and were interested in the ceremonial entrance of the King and Queen to the throne room, the entourage walking backwards before them. By autumn 1912 Lennox, their son, had left Cambridge and set off to take articles in Winnipeg. Their daughter Helen was sent in 1913 to study music in Germany.

More alterations and additions to the house to provide a servants' hall and a back staircase were put in hand. A pair of cottages was built at the same time (presumably a pair in Old Kiln Close). These were both let from July 12th 1913 at 5 shillings per week, with a reduction of 2 pence provided the rent was brought to Chinton Hanger on the same day each week, but there would be no reduction if the rent were delayed or if it had to be collected. Susie's intention was to build another pair of cottages at once to be completed by the time they returned from visiting their son in Canada and she planned to build a further structure described as a small convalescent home for convalescent mothers.

Sir Walter Napier

Shortly afterwards a matron was engaged.

On February 13th 1914 their daughter Helen, safely home in England, was presented at court by Susie who also presented a Mrs Savile.

By the time the next episode of the Family Chronicle was due, the first World War had broken out. The Churt correspondent referred to the small town of tents on Frensham Common with 8,000 men already there, some in khaki some in scarlet uniforms. She explained that economy had become the priority at Chinton Hanger, in food and light but not in labour, though admitted there were problems over the dressmaker's orders being cancelled. Outdoor staff were depleted as the garden boy enlisted, the head gardener was on standby ready to go, though another man, too deaf for war service, remained. A working party of village women knitted mittens whilst Susie read them extracts from the newspapers.

As a form of war service Susie Napier worked 4 nights a week in the large recreation tents on the common assisted on Monday nights by her husband. A good many officers went to Chinton Hanger for a bath and the house was used as a convalescent home for a small number of officers. In July 1915 the quarterly letter to the Chronicle commented that the cottage home was running smoothly with a regular supply of mothers from Commercial Road, East London.

Sir Walter was able to acquire large quantities of manure from the horses and mules left at Frensham Camp after the infantry had departed for the Dardanelles.

Emily Ann Simon, editor of the Family Chronicle, reported in April 1916 that she had turned Lawnhurst, her home at Didsbury, Manchester, into a hospital sleeping 44 whilst she retained very limited accommodation for herself.

Lawnhurst, home of Emily Ann Simon, editor of the Family Chronicle, before it became a hospital in World War I

By March 1916 Lennox Napier had gained his commission in the Canadian army and was in England, stationed at Bramshott Camp. Where formerly there was merely the London road running through it, now there were rows and rows of huts, an "electric light works," a lot of shops and a cinema. Washing facilities were at first so poor that 200 Glasgow students, who had enlisted together, bared themselves in a thunderstorm to get clean.

The war continued, with Walter going up to London each Monday and returning each Friday to fulfil his duties at the War Trade Intelligence Department.

The strains of war with its shortages of staff, including the loss of a secretary to type the Chronicle, prompted its editor in April 1917 to ask if it should be continued. The members voted almost unanimously yes, many apologising for their tardiness in writing each quarter. But eventually it ceased. The strain of the many deaths sustained in the extended family became too much for Emily who lost three of her sons fighting for England; in despair she discontinued the Chronicle.

At that point details of life at Chinton Hanger revert to memories of people who knew the Napiers or to accounts in village documents.

A rather macabre incident is recorded in 1927 when the school authorities allowed the children to be experimented on. In the words of the School Minute Book: "By the generosity of Lady Napier, Vitaglass – by which there is a concentration of violet rays – is being installed in the infant room. We shall watch with interest the effect of this experiment on the health of the children". Nothing more was ever written about the experiment.

Sir Walter's involvement in the village included serving as Chairman of the Recreation Ground Committee, and acting as People's Churchwarden from 1910-1914. At a meeting held at the school in July 1912 he explained the Government's new National Insurance Act introduced by Lloyd George. A further meeting would be required to explain how the Act would affect women, especially domestic servants. In a talk in the new village hall in December 1929 he spoke about the treatment of the Southern Tyrolese by Fascist Italy.

During her life in Churt Susie Napier adopted the role of an English Lady of the Manor, to the amusement of other Churt inhabitants. Some of her remarks seem rather tactless and have gone down in local folk lore. Addressing Cred Thorne, a schoolgirl who had just gained a scholarship to Alton High School: "Where shall we find our servants if the likes of you are educated?" To

Lady Napier

a shop assistant she asked "Do you know who I am? Then address me as M'Lady." Strong men quailed and hid when she was known to be visiting the villagers. A kind observer, Ruth Deadman, summed her up as a woman who meant well but was altogether too interfering.

Her end was tragic; in 1946 a year after her husband's death Susie was crushed to death by a tanker in her own drive. In later years a grandson was murdered in London. After the death of Lady Napier Chinton Hanger was sold to Mr Adamson for £8,000.

The village church has a memorial plaque to Sir Walter and Lady Napier.

There are brief references to two further big houses in Churt.

Churt Lea

A tiny glimpse of the complexities of living in two houses at the start of

Mr and Mrs Allen of Churt Lea
in 1925 when James was 93
and Frances Mary was 83

the 20th Century is seen in a brief letter from Mrs Allen of Churt Lea to a member of her staff at Churt. Mr & Mrs Allen were Quakers, and were in residence at Churt Lea in 1908 though each winter they moved to their home in Croydon. They owned cottages for their staff, including Outmoor where Bantock, one of their two gardeners, lived and Moorside Cottages (then known as Mead End) where the Deadmans lived.

Writing an undated letter from Croydon Mrs Allen instructs Ruth Larby, one of her maids at Churt, in the preparations necessary for the family's return in the third week of February:

"I don't think any of the carpets need come up except the passage, stairs and hall, and a new carpet in the Sheraton room. There will be no white-washing or painting. I expect the motor lorry can come for our luggage, and I expect Miss Fanny [one of her two daughters] and Father will come that day. Ayling [a male servant] and Nelly could come on 20th, the little maid on the 22nd and

Edith and T and mother's nurse and Lizzie on the 23rd . The snow and cold has made it hard and uncomfortable in the country. Here, we did not have much snow

You will know better than I how long it will take to get it all ready at Churt Lea. You can leave the studio bedroom and our curtains, if you like, until we are there".

Three of the gardeners at Churt Lea, Cedric Larby on the left

Barford

A sad little line occurs in a biography of her husband, Gilbert Murray, when Lady Mary, eldest daughter of the Earl of Carlisle (whose residence was Castle Howard), is said "to have found the house Barford too much for her". The pair arrived in 1898 and moved away in 1905, leaving their home unsold.

Barford in 1904

3: Churt and the Great War

Churt War Memorial

The Great War, World War I, started almost 100 years ago, in 1914. The assassination by a Serb of the Archduke Franz Ferdinand, heir to the Austro-Hungarian throne, was the excuse for a conflagration in the Balkan tinderbox that was to involve 9 countries within 6 weeks, and a further 7 countries before its close. It was when Belgium was invaded by the Germans on the morning of Monday August 4th that Britain, being bound by her 1839 Treaty to protect Belgian independence, declared war.

The little village of Churt with its 634 inhabitants, was confused. With no radios and only a weekly newspaper each Saturday, the populace was unprepared for the happenings on August Bank Holiday Monday. Abruptly, there was no military band at Headley Flower Show; troops were confined to barracks. On the following day Churt learned the magnitude of the situation when notices in Post Offices and at police stations summoned reservists to the colours. There were many in Churt, eight in the Royal Irish Hussars alone.

Churt's well-loved vicar, A W Watson, wrote in the September village magazine: "Since the last issue of the magazine our country has become in-volved in the greatest war that the world has known for many centuries; it will demand from our country great sacrifices and bring bitter sorrow to many families."

Refugees from Belgium began to arrive in Britain and two families took up residence in Churt. One family of 3 generations was housed in the old Bowles farmhouse at Silverbeck; the other family lived over the garage at Barford, the self-same house used in 1956 by Hungarian refugees.

As early as January 1914 Frensham Parish Council had recorded in its Minute Book rumours of the acquisition of the common by the Military, but the common had frequently been used for manoeuvres, ever since the military authorities bought large tracts of waste land around Aldershot in 1853 for army purposes. The fields off Green Lane were devoted to carrots grown specially for the cavalry horses at Aldershot. Military activity had always been a matter of excitement for the schoolchildren so that absenteeism was frequent on such occasions. Almost overnight Frensham Common became filled with militia, many from the north country. Few of the soldiers had uniforms; many remained in mufti; some were issued with old-stock scarlet uniforms. There was to be a constant flood of men in training before shipment overseas. Encampments arose throughout this western part of Surrey. Kitchener's heart-rending appeal for 1,400,000 volunteers was a priority. Inspections of the troops were the subject of visits from royalty and other dignitaries. By November 1914 49 Churt men

Frensham Camp, 10th September 1914

were serving, and their names were listed in the church porch. Soon afterwards, Miss Abbott erected a board at the corner of the village green with the names of those in the forces, a practice started on London street corners to indicate those serving from that street. Known as "War Shrines" these structures were often surrounded by flowers, banners and slogans. They aroused opposition from some people who regarded them as sacrilegious.

Billeting of soldiers began in 1914 with Hindhead Golf Club-house being used for officers of the King's Royal Rifles. By February 1915 soldiers from a company of the Royal Army Service Corps were billeted in Churt, and a parade service

Witley Camp

was held every Sunday morning at church. Householders had been asked how many soldiers they could take in on a sleeping-only basis, the rate being 6 pence a night for the first man and 4 pence thereafter. The Farnham Herald patriotically wrote: "We would urge all those who have the honour – we repeat honour - of sheltering British soldiers under their roofs to be happy to make them welcome" Churt welcomed these volunteers. The Institute offered free membership; "smoking concerts" were held at the school.

In June that year the church magazine recorded the first fatal casualty among Churt serving men – Sergeant Thomas Clark of the Essex Yeomanry, killed at Ypres. Eight men died from Churt in 1915 and on December 27th St John's Church held a special service for these servicemen killed in action.

The ladies of Churt worked valiantly at making comforts for the services. Lady Meynell at The Chase advised her Red Cross members to continue making shirts, cut out ready for collection from her home. The school asked for wool so that the girls could knit for the combatants. Regularly cash collections were taken at school, the money being sent for the Weekly Dispatch Tobacco Fund, and the children were delighted when postcards of thanks were received from men of various units at the Front.

Temporary hospitals were created locally when Mr Charrington of Frensham Hill (now Frensham Heights School) offered his residence where 22 huts each with 20 beds were erected in the grounds. Mrs Lewin gave up The Hill, Gong Hill, for the same purpose. The latter became known as Hill Military

Hospital. It was to this hospital that Churt sent its fruit and vegetables following the harvest festival service in 1916. The Bishop of Winchester at Farnham Castle offered his home as a hospital and his park as a grazing area for ill-conditioned horses. Waverley Abbey was a hospital frequently visited by royalty. To the south of Churt were three more temporary hospitals: Grayshott Military Hospital, Hilders Military Hospital, (set up in the mansion Hilders on the lower end of Hindhead Hill from Haslemere), and High Rough Hospital, a large Victorian mansion at the top of Farnham Lane, nowadays a school.

Within the Parish of Frensham lay one of the largest riding schools in the country. From 1914-18 this site - Frensham Place - was used by the Royal Army Service Corps as a depot. The owner of Frensham Place was Sir C Arthur Pearson who was later to become blind and to found St Dunstan's Hospital for the Blind. Eventually in 1939 his former home became Edgeborough School.

Frensham Parish Council replied coolly to the request by the Lord Lieutenant of Surrey for committees to be formed in each parish to administer relief if cases of necessity should arise from the war. The Council said they already had many such committees so the Farnham Committee could represent them on the Lord Lieutenant's committee. They did, however, agree to help with recruitment and covered every house in Frensham, Churt and Hindhead.

An unexpected effect of the war shocked Churt in 1915 when the "Lusitania" was sunk by a German submarine off the coast of Ireland with the loss of 1,201 lives. As a result, a whole family from the village was wiped out when the parents, six children and their nanny from Romney Lodge (now Churt House) were lost at sea.

German prisoners of war, held near Frimley and other local sites, queued weekly at Churt Post Office at Jumps Road to look for mail. With them they brought home–made shoe horns and buttonhooks to sell, one of which is in Ruth Deadman's possession to this day.

The Parish Council in 1915 agreed to join surrounding parishes to procure a motor fire engine in place of their existing horse drawn machine. This obviously did not come to pass because in December 1917, when Farnham had the effrontery to ask Frensham for a donation to the Joint Fire Brigade, Frensham refused until their services were extended to this parish, a deed finally accomplished in March 1918.

National Egg Collection Week took place in March 1916 and Churt

schoolchildren provided 100 eggs for the wounded. The Chancellor of the Exchequer launched his Victory War Loan in 1916. By this time the school had formed a War Savings Association affiliated to the County War Savings Committee. Under the Cultivation of Lands Order 1916, the authorities were to requisition land for food production but when three parishioners asked the Council to provide allotments the Council declined, saying the demand was too small. The government issued declarations which citizens were expected to sign: "*I realise that economy in the use of all food and checking of all waste helps our country to complete victory. I promise as far as I possibly can to follow out ration instructions and suggestions issued by the food controller . . . All food savers are active allies to the men in the trenches*".

The government summoned representatives of all Surrey golf clubs to Whitehall in 1915 to consider ploughing up the ground for food production. Hindhead Golf Club was considered unsuitable.

Householders were asked to let their parish councillors know how many seed potatoes they required for the following year, so in April 1917 the Council took delivery of 40 cwt (hundredweight) of seed potatoes some of which, complained a Spreakley parishioner, were small and rotten.

Regularly the church magazine listed the names of those fallen in action. In August 1917 it recorded the award of the Military Medal to Private Frank Bowers of the 2nd East Surrey Regiment, and in October 1918 we learned that Private George Bantock had also received an MM.

Before it left for overseas service the 125th Battalion of Canadian Infantry laid up its colours in St John's Church on May 12th 1917 in a moving service attended by the Bishop of Winchester. At the service a letter was read from Mr Watson the vicar, on his bed of sickness. It was his last act as vicar of Churt, as he died on May 21st. A later vicar was to remark on the joy derived from "our young Canadians' sacred songs". Over the many years of encampment on the common beautiful gardens developed around the Officers' Mess and it became a regular Sunday event for Churt residents to look round them.

Depositing of the Canadian Colours on May 12th 1917 in the 'quaint Parish Church at Churt, Surrey'

The munitions factory at Frensham aroused ireful complaints from local residents who detested its noisy hooter.

Churt's vicar designate, the Rev D R Barton, was serving as a chaplain to the forces and had to wait until April 10th 1918 before he could take up his duties at Churt. Nevertheless, only six months later in October, he informed parishioners that he had taken a part-time job of war work, acting as foreman supervising the loading of pit props (a familiar use of wood from Churt). He declared :- *Under the present conditions of scarcity of labour I am satisfied that I am right in doing this.*

In all the struggles of a protracted war, Churt had a unique part to play in one respect – the estate of Silverbeck was used three times in 1915 as a training ground for the United Arts Rifles.

The United Arts Rifles was one of the first Volunteer Corps to be formed at the outbreak of war and consisted of members of the artistic professions in London. *"The sculptor flung down his chisel, the painter his brushes, the writer his pen, the musician his instrument, the actor the buskin"* - a motley though distinguished group, which occasioned the remark, "Everyone will admire their patriotism, but is there not a fear that their very originality will be their undoing?" The Corps was almost a copy of the Roll of Fame in English Art – painters, architects, sculptors, authors, poets, journalists, singers, novelists. Names such as Sir Hubert Parry, Sir Herbert Beerbohm Tree, Sir Charles Stanford, G Lethaby (architect of Watts Chapel at Compton, Surrey) were included in the muster.

Battalion Parade, August 1915

The connection with Churt was, of course, Bryan Hook RA, painter son of James Clark Hook, RA, who had built Silverbeck in 1866. Bryan held the rank of Lieutenant RN and had a son serving in the regular forces but was keen to be of use to this Corps which, for many months, the military authorities were

The Unshrinkables, November 1914

not interested in. Until Kitchener's demand for men was met, these rakish volunteers were of little significance to the authorities. They had no equipment, no uniforms, so they bought their own white sweaters and were known as The Unshrinkables, Their appearance prompted onlookers to believe they were German prisoners, convicts, scouts, even celebrated Russians from Archangel – anything but soldiers. Their first weapons were provided at the expense of the battalion – collectors' pieces, which might have been deadly weapons if the bullet left the muzzle, in which case anything it hit must die of blood poisoning. Each weapon was bought by the volunteers, or hired at 6 shillings per annum.

A participant at one of these Camps wrote:

"The Easter, Whit and Summer camps of 1915 were held at Churt where Mr Bryan Hook, then Musketry Instructor to the corps, placed his estate at the disposal of the corps. Camp involved strenuous days on Frensham Common, long route marches over Hind Head, bridge building, trench digging and shooting at Mr Hook's ingenious 100 yards' range."

Officers, Churt, 1915.
(Bryan Hook is ringed)

A later Commandant was to marvel at the spirit of the older men, whose most strenuous exertion for years had been a round of golf, who ordinarily would not walk 500 yards in London if a taxi-cab were available yet there they were swinging along like boys in a 20-mile march, or breasting the sandy slopes above Frensham Pond with the vigour of youth. Used to every comfort and luxury of the best London Clubs they slept uncomplainingly on the stone floor of Churt Schoolhouse. Others were billeted over the stables at Silverbeck.

"D" Company Quarters, School House, Churt
August 1915

On another occasion the Corps was inspected by a well-known General who stopped dead behind a private whose luxuriant tresses would have graced any lady of the ballet – *"Deary me, deary me, I suppose it can't be helped, they ARE volunteers."*

The incident resulted in a comment from one of the writers –

Is it a boy? Is it a girl?
Is it a nut or a precious pearl?
Is it a freak, is it quite sane ?
Who does his hair when he goes on campaign?

The War Office took control of the Corps in autumn 1916. This brought to an end its nebulous and semi-official life and ended two years of official neglect. Ultimately, it was recognised by its being affiliated to the Central Association of Volunteer Training Corps. Gradually leaders of the various professions dropped out one by one through inanition or avoirdupois, but younger replacements were active in manning aircraft guns in London. Some were sent abroad; two officers serving overseas at Arras in 1917 exchanged

memories of "5 squirts rapid" from the publican near the schools in Churt.

By 1918 they were considered to be a more efficient fighting unit than many units sent to France in the earliest days.

By 1918 the whole nation was growing weary after four years of war; nevertheless what was to become its last year started fiercely in Spring with a German offensive designed to inflict a knockout blow. It was not to succeed.

Recognition was given in April 1918 to the flying men of Britain and the name Royal Air Force adopted. Ultimately, hostilities ceased with the Armistice on November 11th 1918, at the 11th hour of the 11th day of the 11th month. It was said that not a foot of German home territory had been directly taken by Allied forces. This belief led the Germans to view the war not as defeat but as betrayal, an interpretation which contributed to events 21 years later.

As to how Churt learned the news there is no record. Certainly Farnham was uncertain. There were rumours early in the morning that the troops at Aldershot had knocked off for the day and were already painting the town red. Even Reuters Agency was unable to confirm rumours of the peace. Our little village finally recognised that the long, drawn-out anguish of war was over; spontaneously residents made their way to the church for a service of thanksgiving.

The Roll of Honour in the magazine had listed 13 names and mentioned two winners of the Military Medal: Private Frank Bowers in August 1917 and Private George Bantock in October 1918. Our present war memorial has 20 names inscribed on it relating to the dead of the Great War, all from Churt ecclesiastical parish.

The recreation ground is the village's memorial to those lost in World War I. Inside the church is the Watts memorial panel in the chancel. But the war memorial on the village green had to wait till the end of World War II for belated recognition.

After the formal signing of the Peace Treaty in July 1919 the whole country rejoiced in a month of national celebrations. Not least was Churt's magnificent firework display, the gift of the Keep family who lived at Prairie Cottage, (now Hopton, in Jumps Road).

Patricks, stonemasons of Farnham, were commissioned to carve the names of the fallen on tablets throughout the world – Jerusalem, Baghdad, New Zealand, the Menin Gate at Ypres. Careful examination reveals the initials HCP on them.

Relating people to their memorial

The Larbys as children

MEN OF CHURT WHO DIED
THAT HONOUR MIGHT LIVE
1914 - 1918

ARCHIE BOWERS PTE. E. SURREY REGT
FRANK BOWERS PTE. THE QUEEN'S
H.J. CANE PTE. ROYAL FUS.
JAMES CLARK PTE. M.T. CORPS
THOMAS CLARK SERGT. ESSEX YEO
A.T.W. CONSTABLE MAJOR ESSEX REGT.
L.A. CRIDDLE PTE. THE QUEEN'S
H.E. GOODYEAR H.M.S. BLACK PRINCE
ERNEST HARRIS PTE. R.A.S.C.
DUNCAN HOOK 2ND LIEUT. LANCS FUS.
ROBIN HOOK 2ND LIEUT. LANCS FUS.
VALENTINE HOOK CAPT. THE QUEEN'S
....E. HUTCHINGS.... PTE. MIDDX. REGT.
CEDRIC LARBY PTE. LONDON REGT.
HERBERT LARBY PTE. HANTS REGT.
THOMAS LARBY PTE. THE QUEEN'S

Cedric Larby

Herbert Larby

Thomas Larby

Col; Smythe's answer to letter

reference to your letter garding 6352 Rfm C. Larby gret to have to inform you was Killed by a shell hilst carrying a machine gn into action. This occurred hilst the Batt. was at the Somme

Notification of Cedric Larby's death in battle

IN LOVING MEMORY
OF

THOMAS LARBY,

(Private 3rd Queens).

Killed in Action in France, July 19th, 1915,

AGED 28 YEARS.

Gone from us, but not forgotten,
Never shall his memory fade,
Sweetest thoughts shall ever linger

36

4: How Churt Acquired its Recreation Ground

Churt Recreation Ground on Fete day, 2000

Within a fortnight of the cessation of the Great War, Churt held two public meetings to decide upon a war memorial to commemorate Churt men who had lost their lives in the conflict. It was agreed to create a recreation ground and to purchase the 10-acre Crossways Field adjoining the Institute. Five and a half acres were to be reserved for public recreation, the remaining area would be divided into quarter-acre building plots and be made available to ex-servicemen. The executors of Mr C E C Prichard of Llanover (died 1908) and of his wife (died 1917) agreed to accept £800 for the land. (Mr Prichard had been listed as one of Churt's principal landowners in 1899, together with Lord Ashcombe, Mr J C Hook and Mr Trimmer.) Straightway an appeal for £850 was launched and the vicar, Mr Barton, appointed sole trustee of all monies collected.

There were at least 75 ex-servicemen to be considered for the building plots, four of which were to be reserved for shops. A rigorous definition of "Churt Men" was minuted. Each quarter acre plot was to cost £20 with conveyancing costs covered by the trustees out of a common fund. If there were insufficient plots, length of residence in Churt would give preference; if any plots remained unsold they were to be offered to Churt residents.

Six months later in April 1919 the first report was made to the residents when the vicar announced that £1,000. 8s.0d had been raised. Unfortunately there had been two problems. Firstly, the vendors discovered that the land, unknown to them, had been let by Surrey Agricultural Commissioners to a neighbouring farmer on a 3 year lease and, secondly, a third of an acre had already been sold to Mr James Alan Croucher in 1916 for a workshop. Both difficulties were overcome: the farmer accepted £10 compensation, and Mr Croucher agreed to an exchange of land of equal area. At the same meeting four additional persons were appointed as trustees to the War Memorial Charity and their terms agreed. They were all aware that a tithe had to be paid on the land.

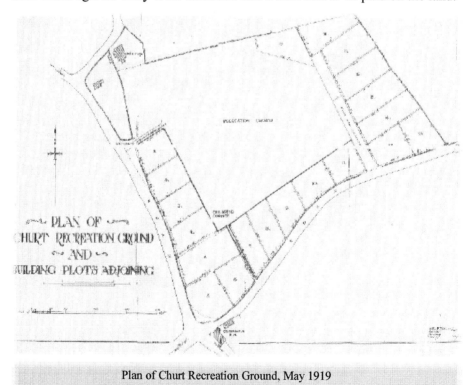

Plan of Churt Recreation Ground, May 1919

The five trustees, Messrs Barton (vicar), Keep, Baker, Harris and Mitchell became responsible for the land purchased with the monies collected. In 1922 the Charity Commission formally recognised these five gentlemen, together with Mr Martin, as the trustees of the land to be known as Churt Recreation Ground.

Purchasers of the building plots had to agree not to let the plots to gypsies or squatters nor to use them for business purposes. Part of the field at the corner of Hale House Lane was to be given to the Council for road widening. In 1922 the trustees further agreed that one plot for a village hall was to be reserved for a further 5-year period.

The returning servicemen had high hopes that they could have a bowling green. In addition they had their plans for the New Institute which had been built in 1909, superseding a much older structure, on land given by Mr Prichard who had not lived to see it opened. During the war servicemen camping on Frensham Common had been made welcome at the Institute. Now, after the war, members were to lease the Institute at a peppercorn rent and name it The Working Men's Club, which they planned to run themselves as "an experiment in self-government".

Most building plots were sold within a few months though plots 5 and 6, on the corner and designed to be sold as one unit, remained unsold until May 1921 when Mr Stone bought them for £150.

In July 1919 Mr Abbott of Beefolds bought a plot for himself, presumably for housing his domestic staff, and ear-marked plot 7 for use as a school garden. This school garden was conveyed on 6th March 1920 by the Recreation Ground Trustees to the School Managers, namely, the Vicar, Col. Smythe of Barford, Mr Hurry of Llanover and Mrs Bessie Harris. The names of the original purchasers of building plots are listed in the Recreation Ground Minute Book.

Two matters are puzzling. How did an ordinary resident, Mr Abbott, manage to buy himself a plot so early in the sale? Is there a clue in 1954 when Admiral Sir William James wrote an obituary for Mrs Abbott in the village magazine, saying that "Our fine recreation ground was their gift"? Perhaps they were the most generous donors and were deemed to have a priority on a plot. The second puzzle occurs when, in 1925, a tithe rent charge was demanded of the trustees. At that point Sir Walter Napier (appointed a trustee in September 1925) agreed to pay arrears of tithe owed by his wife. As Lady Napier was not named on the original list of purchasers she must have obtained the plot(s) from an earlier purchaser.

Much work was needed to bring the original field into condition as a recreation ground; levelling (a steam roller was used), grass sowing, turf laying, construction of a grass tennis court, and development of a small area behind the

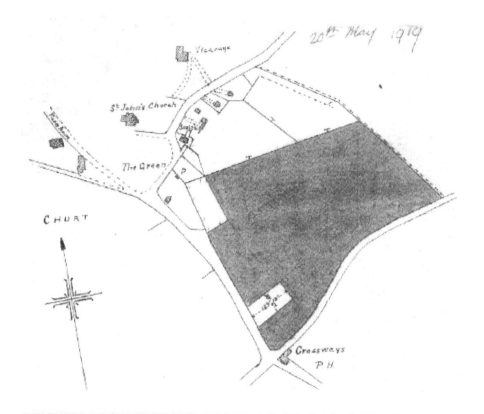

Second plan of Churt Recreation Ground, 20th May 1919

present village hall for use as a children's playground. By August 1920 a pavilion had been provided by Mr Abbott who bought one of the many ex-army huts available. Later, in 1922, he was thanked for providing the memorial gates and gate-posts with the names of the fallen inscribed upon them. Ever cautious about expenditure, the trustees asked if Mr Wolfe would graze his sheep on the grounds but when he declined they accepted that the grass would have to be cut by pony mower or by a machine – if they could afford one.

A fancy dress group celebrates the opening of the pavilion in 1920. Back row: starting at 5th left, is Eric Larby, Dorothy Martin and Bert Matthews. 2nd back row: 5th from left is Mrs Glaysher (neé Karn) 3rd row:, next to woman in tall hat, is Gertrude Martin. 4th, further along in centre is Harry Massey. Next row: 2nd left is Olive Larby - wife of Eric - dressed as a farmer. Front row: all unknown

Alterations to the original Trust Deed were initiated in 1922 when the legal estate of the ground was vested in the Official Trustee of Charitable Lands. From then, control of the recreation ground was in the hands of 6 trustees, supported by a committee of management comprising 2 representatives each from the cricket, football and tennis clubs, plus 3 co-opted members.

In 1925 the trustees sought to redeem the tithe, so they asked the Board of Agriculture how much the redemption money would be. The required sum of £91.14s 0d was paid partly out of remaining funds and partly from gifts from the trustees themselves.

The last remaining plot of land was conveyed by the Board of Charity Commissioners to Mr Mason, Mr Bosanquet (vicar), Mr Lloyd George, Col. H Smythe and Mr Szlumper in February 1928 as a site for a village hall, which was officially opened in November of that year. The need for a village hall had first been emphasised by Churt's vicar in the 1890s, followed by many other pleas after that.

The development of a recreation ground and the building of new homes, shops and a village hall so transformed Churt that the centre was moved from "St. Martin's Square" (at the end of Jumps Road) to its present site.

The above account completes the tale of how Churt acquired its recreation ground. It is now so much an essential part of Churt life that a few further events should be noted.

There still remained a need for a bowling green. In 1929 the Working Men's Club asked for a bowling green but the committee replied that funds did not permit it. In 1962, after Frensham Parish Council had taken over responsibility for Churt ward's recreation ground, a request by Mr R Sylvester that residents of Churt be permitted to use Frensham bowling green was turned down.

The pavilion in 1934

A public meeting in March 1939 had voted against a proposal that the Frensham Parish Council be asked to take over the recreation ground. The Management Committee had argued, and the Trustees supported their argument, that despite an annual appeal for money over and above the income from the sports clubs' rents, there were insufficient funds to maintain the ground at the desired standard. They deemed it would be fairer if every ratepayer contributed towards its upkeep as it was a facility for the general public, not merely for the sports clubs. Eventually, in 1962, after a further public meeting, a transfer was agreed. The

Groundsman John Marshall

six trustees of Churt Recreation Ground were discharged, at their own request, and Frensham Parish Council was appointed in their place. When Churt formed its own parish council in 2003, the Charity Commissioners were asked to agree to the transfer of the trusteeship from Frensham to Churt Parish Council.

Tony and Penelope Barnsdale

The 1960s saw a new pavilion, with running water, electricity and waterborne sanitation, being erected with the help of much voluntary labour.

In the 1980s Mrs Milva Sandison and a group of dedicated parents provided a new, large play area for the children on a different site.

In the same decade Mr & Mrs Barnsdale made a substantial contribution to two new hard tennis courts. Shortly afterwards members of the tennis club constructed a paved seating area and erected their own pavilion on the exact site where the first tennis pavilion had existed.

The recreation ground has again become the site of Churt's annual fete, an event having its roots in the Annual Flower Show which originally was held in the grounds of various larger houses.

Today the public recreation ground serves the purpose for which it was designed, as an area for Churt people to stroll and relax in, as a playground for the children and as a venue for sportsmen in cricket, football and tennis, all of whom have sections devoted to coaching youth. Perhaps one day a still-wanted bowling green will be accommodated.

Junior tennis coaching at the Recreation Ground today

Young cricketers in training

5: The Edwin Abbott Memorial Cottages

Star Hill Chapel, c.1880

Churt's "almshouses" are situated at Star Hill. They were the benefaction of the Abbott family to commemorate the death in 1932 of Edwin Abbott of Beefolds.

In 1909 the Abbotts had moved to the property now known as Threeways, but then called Beefolds, which they had bought from Mr Bryan Hook who had moved into Silverbeck, his late father's home. The conveyance of their property included the old chapel at Star Hill and its adjoining land.

Later Mr & Mrs Abbott had a new house built on what is now the A287, nearer the Great Pond and took the name Beefolds with them. Further branches of the Abbott family lived in Frensham, at Birchen Hey and at Hammondswood.

Over the years Mr Abbott had been generous to Churt in many ways, particularly to its children whom he took to Aldershot pantomime at Christmas and for whom he always had a handful of sweets as they came out of school. During the First World War any serviceman on leave was expected to call on him before returning to duty and to receive a crisp ten shilling note. He was an outspoken man and was surprised at the answer to his question, "Are you an honest man, Croucher?" The answer came, "An honest man grows hairs on the palm of his hand".

Beefolds, 1909

In 1919 he reserved one of the plots of land on offer to ex-servicemen, and ensured that the School Managers acquired it for a school garden. He provided the first pavilion on the new recreation ground and paid for the gates and gate posts where the names of Churt's fallen in the Great War are engraved.

Star Hill Chapel, converted to staff cottages by Mr Abbott.
They were named Beefold Cottages

After Edwin Abbott's death in September 1932 five members of the family – trustees of the venture – met in April 1933 at Beefolds having earlier decided that, at their joint expense, they would erect two cottages in his memory on land adjoining the former chapel. The cottages were to be available to those in need. In addition, the trustees aimed to create an endowment fund, each member having to subscribe to it. Their enterprise was registered as a charity.

Edwin Abbott Memorial Cottages, 1933

At first the premises were very simple. Though they had iron curtain rods made by Karn, Churt's blacksmith, and Welsh dressers constructed by Chuters, who had built the cottages, there was no gas or electricity. Later, one tenant trying to heat her room with an oil stove severely burned herself. Gas and electricity, with two power points per cottage, arrived in 1947 and in 1956 three extra points per cottage were installed.

The original requirements, which applicants had to satisfy in order to become tenants, were stringent. Their income was not to exceed £40 p.a.; they were not to absent themselves for more than a fortnight each year without the approval of the trustees; they later had to request permission to install a television set given to them.

Upon the opening of the cottages, a Miss Smith had the sole occupancy of cottage number 1 until her death in 1950 but, thereafter, the trustees attempted to have both cottages continually occupied by two persons. Thus, when Mr Deadman died in cottage number 2, having lived there three years with his wife, his widow was expected to share her home with another, unknown, occupant. She preferred to live with relatives.

By 1957, following the death of two trustees, the remaining trustees sought means whereby the future of the cottages could be put on a firm, lasting foundation. After correspondence with the Charity Commissioners, they asked the District Council, in those days Hambledon, to become involved. Thus, on Christmas Eve 1959 the Old Trustees held their final meeting and the new Board of Trustees took over.

Since that time the Charity Commissioners have been approached, and the conditions of tenancy today are widely different, The cottages remain an attractive reminder of a popular Churt family.

6: Quinnettes in the 1930s

For more than seven decades a tattered cluster of pages, with hardly distinguishable photographs, has been passed from hand to hand in Churt. This seems an opportune moment to preserve them, for they comprise an article which appeared in some unidentified magazine of the 1930s, enthusing over the alterations to Quinnettes made by Mrs Palin-Evans, its then owner.

Quinnettes, pre-1927, when the old Mediaeval house was divided into three cottages

It is generally known that Quinnettes was an original three-bay Mediaeval house which eventually was converted into three labourers' cottages. Then around 1920 Commander White bought the cottages and restored them to one dwelling. By autumn 1928 Mrs Palin- Evans, a widow with two sons, had bought the property. She immediately began alterations enabling the family to move in during summer 1929. Apart from the garden features scarcely shown here, there was a tennis court and a croquet lawn.

The captions to the following illustrations, taken from the magazine, show Quinnettes during the Palin-Evans' occupation until they left in 1935 for The Rookery at Frensham. The literary style is journalese of the 1930s.

Quinnettes garden in the 1930s

Quinnettes in the 1930s

Seen on the left is the lovely old barn, which is one of the finest examples of a Cambrian hooded barn in existence. Note the sweep of the expansive roof and the picturesque gable over the porch. On the right is a winding, stone-flagged path which makes its way between a beautiful rock garden now carpeted with blue gentian.

In the lounge the floor is on two levels as it has been formed by throwing the old living-room, scullery and back premises into one. The carpet and hangings are a soft green shade which makes an attractive accompaniment to walls of pale biscuit and Jacobean chintzes which are used to cover the chairs and settee. In the background one catches a glimpse of the entrance hall with its beautifully designed grille gate.

One important feature of this room is the lovely old inglenook and brick-tiled fireplace framed in with massive oak beams. The arched niches on either side are lit by concealed lights which silhouette the small armour models.

Another view of the lounge, looking towards the dining-room. The beamed ceiling is in a beautiful state of preservation and unusual lighting effects are obtained by concealed lighting framed in old oak and built round the principal supports. Note the fine example of a 14th Century chest by the door.

Left, a closer view of the south side of the house, show-ing the loggia in more detail, the west wall of which forms the back of an open air aviary for vivid plumaged budgeri-gars.

Mrs Palin-Evans' own bedroom is a study in delicate and exqui-site shades with graceful con-tours to the furniture. The walls and ceilings have been "Surfexed" shading from silver to turquoise blue. A striking contrast is given by the hang-ings and carpet of deep salmon pink, whilst the beautiful bed and dressing table are carried out in pale blue lacquer with pink sea anemones in relief.

The distinctive feature of this bedroom is the magnificent old oak four-poster. A carpet of bright cherry red and a French chintz in yellow, mauve and cherry give a richness and depth of colour particularly in keeping with the atmosphere of the room and emphasise the beautifully wrought carving and weathered dignity of the furniture.

In the dining room the walls have been treated in a rough silver which throws the old oak beams and antique furniture into a striking relief. A rich shade of burnt orange is used for the carpet and curtains. The fine, massive refectory table terminates in an ancient King Post at the far end.

53

A more modern, aerial view of Quinnettes in the second half of the Twentieth Century

7: Farming on the Lloyd George Estate

Lloyd George, no doubt, when his time runs out
Will ride in a blazing chariot
Drawn in state on a red-hot plate
By Satan and Judas Iscariot

Ananias that day will be heard to say
"My claim to precedence fails,
Stand back from the fire and stoke up the pyre,
Make way for the liar from Wales"

The rhyme above was going the rounds of the London Clubs in the early 1900s. Lloyd George's popularity was far from universal; the poor may have referred to him as Lord George (believing that a man so great and good could be no mere commoner) but his 1909 Budget, with its provisions for death duties, supertax, and land value duties, was a Budget designed in effect to make a complete evaluation of the land of Great Britain. It alarmed and alienated the landowners.

Lloyd George by Low

When in 1921 she was house-hunting for Lloyd George, his secretary Frances Stevenson became aware that Lord Ashcombe's estate was on the market. The ex-Prime Minister having approved of the general location, 60 acres were bought at a favourable price of £3,000 and the house Bron-y-de was built. Regularly more land was acquired as it became available, with LG keeping the land but selling the farmhouses attached. His interest was in food production and his experiments with fruit farming included the sounding of bells when frost was imminent so that his employees got up at night and lit small containers of paraffin (known as smudge pots) under the trees. It is said that this practice stopped in the war when the metal containers were commandeered. At the outbreak of World War II in 1939 Lloyd George was the largest employer in the neighbourhood and was held in high esteem by his farmworkers who were paid more than the nego-

Landgirls

tiated wages for agricultural workers; they received £2 2s per week instead of the statutory £1 11s 6d. The workers' cottages built by him were the first in Churt to have hot and cold running water. Despite agriculture being a "Reserved Occupation" many men left for the forces, so that tending the land and the nation's food supplies, depended significantly on landgirls.

Three living memoires of working on Lloyd George's estate are recounted here, two from landgirls, one from their male foreman.

Eve Petty

At the outbreak of war Eve Petty was living with her family in Upper Norwood. She joined the Women's Land Army, much to her parents' dismay, for landgirls were believed to be tough and rough. Some were, she says, but the differing backgrounds added a fascinating variety to the teams. Eve, being a violinist, was held in some awe and was promptly nicknamed The Old Fiddler.

A landgirl's uniform consisted of boots, Wellington boots, shoes, socks, one jumper, breeches, shirt, dungarees with a bib front, an overcoat "for best" and a brimmed hat.

For her first job Eve was sent to the Officers' Rest Home in Farnham, opposite the

Eve Petty

railway station, where she was in charge of the flower beds with not a vegetable in sight. Before long, she was drafted to a group organisation which sent landgirls wherever they were needed. Thus, she arrived at the fruit farm where Lloyd George needed his fruit trees spraying with a tar-oil winter wash. The chosen girls were all darkhaired and as many as possible were dark-

Landgirls in the canteen at Lloyd George's farm

skinned. Protective clothing was provided but, obviously, the authorities deemed it too precarious for girls with fair colouring. At their lunchbreak Lloyd George would appear in his cloak and sit with the landgirls. For three winters Eve returned to this task.

Eve's several billets were uninspiring. Washing was done in cold water; food in the digs doesn't bear recalling. Every so often extra rations were issued to landgirls to sustain their physical work; they received an extra pound of sugar, extra cheese and jam, and a small quantity of butter. But the issue of their clothing was erratic. At first Eve had baggy corded breeches - in a size too large for her small build - a green jersey, green shirt, a pull-on hat like a trilby, shoes, but no wellingtons. Two winters were to pass before she was provided with an overcoat. Her take-home wages were 11s 6d per week (60 pence) after paying £1 per week for board and lodging.

At other seasons Eve was employed on various farms. She remembers her employers at Secretts off the Hog's

Mr Lloyd George's farm shop, opposite the Pride of the Valley

Back as slavedrivers,

where the girls picked ice-covered sprouts with no gloves and where even permission "to spend a penny" had to be sought. But other jobs are still remembered as fun. There was the time when she and another girl had to look after sheep on Wentworth Golf Course. There were 500 sheep and the two girls, living in a caravan at the time, had to count them in and count them out as they opened and shut the gate each day. The farmer provided each girl with sharp knives to tend to the hooves when the weather was very wet.

Knives were dubious tools. A job in Epsom involved pigs. Three or four girls were each given a sharp knife to castrate piglets. But where? How? A certain number of Eve's piglets died; perhaps they were sows, not boars? Sickles were issued for hedging and ditching but not gloves – the landgirls were expected to buy their own. Their layered hedge at Witley and their ditching were proof of consummate skill. On one occasion the girls were delivered by cart to a farm to start clearing the ditches. At the end of a long, hard day it was discovered that the driver had dropped them at the wrong farm, but the farmer was delighted at the unexpected bonus!

Harvest time was dirty, dusty and filthy work. There were few harvesting machines but, wherever a machine was hired, the landgirls would rake out

all the husks and rubbish from under the throbbing machine with a big wooden rake, on to a canvas sheet, bundling it up and carting it off to be burnt. They finished up as black as coalmen, eyes, nose, mouth and ears choked with dust. Eve had quickly picked up the skill of tractor driving and so was the envy of her co-workers. She also drove the tractor for potato harvest on a number of occasions. Less happy was her experience with an enormous cart-horse, which trod on her foot resulting in hospitalisation at Guildford.

Feeding time at Mr Lloyd George's farm, Churt

The war over, Eve returned to her office work in London, but quickly wearied of being indoors. She left for Cornwall where she joined a French couple in establishing a bulb farm after they had been bombed out of London. At that time German POWs, not yet repatriated, helped to plant these acres of land. The cumbersome boxes of cut flowers were balanced precariously on Eve's bike as she took them to the funny old bus for the journey to the station and beyond.

Eve in 2004

Some wartime friendships lasted a short time, others were more durable. Lillian Braund, a friend from Eve's landgirl days, married a Clovelly man. Together the couple created a garden of many acres, full of rare shrubs and plants at Whimple in Devon where hundreds of keen gardeners visit each year. The agricultural skills learned by the girls of the Land Army resulted in many fine gardeners, of whom Eve is one in Churt.

Gwynne Chuter

Gwynne in 2004

Different memories of that period come from Gwynne Chuter of Frensham who, on reaching school leaving age, was expected to take up war work so she sought work on the land. Mr Caro of Barford Court, Churt, employed landgirls but, having no vacancies at the time of her enquiry, directed her to Lloyd George's agent who offered her work in the greenhouses used for tomatoes and salad crops. The Lloyd George agricultural estate covered glasshouses, orchards, arable crops, a piggery, soft fruit and beekeeping, this last being in the charge of Miss Parry, LG's former secretary living at Stream Cottage. The hives were scattered widely over Hankley Common.

Gwynne recalls her companions - Winnie Bance from Portsmouth, Doreen Sandberg from Hull, Foreman Bland, Under Foreman Tom Booker, Old Mr Parr, Clarence from the Channel Islands and Violet Skates who lived at Beacon Hill. Then Nonie from Croydon arrived and lodged with the Weatherleys at Lovett in Hale House Lane. At a later date, as German bombing took its toll, Winnie's parents, Mr & Mrs

Gwynne Chuter (centre)

Bance, were moved from their coastal home at Portsmouth and found some farm cottages, Penrhos, in Green Lane, Churt. A little later Nonie's mother was bombed out of Croydon so LG provided her with accommodation at Silver Birch Cottages in Hyde Lane. Country life, however, was not her style so she returned as soon as she was able. Fifty years or more afterwards, photos of Winnie Bance and Nonie Moresi were to appear on the cover of a book about Churt, "Churt Remembered".

Lloyd George and staff

el: Hindhead 28.
Station: Farnham.

Bron-y-de,
Churt,
Surrey.

To whom it may concern,

Thomas Carter has been employed as Gardener by the Rt. Hon. D. Lloyd George for over sixteen years. He has always proved himself to be honest, sober, and very hard-working. He has had a great deal to do, and has performed it conscientiously. He is leaving at his own request.

F. L. Stevenson.

Secretary.

A reference written by Frances Stevenson for one of Lloyd George's employees, Thomas Carter

Transport was invariably horse drawn. Joey was a pony that pulled the small cart used for delivering vegetables. Nonie Moresi, its driver, had to collect the produce carefully laid out at the side of the fields, fill her cart and deliver the crop. On one occasion the deafening noise from a line of tanks frightened her pony. Standing ("like Boadicea in her chariot", she said) she raised her hand, stopped the queue and crossed the track before calmly indicating that the tanks could proceed. Her first digs were rather rustic, with no electricity, baths limited to one a week, the light turned off at exactly the same time each night. Later she resided with the shoemaker, Mr Weatherley of Lovett, Hale House Lane.

The extra food ration granted around harvest time did little to assuage the hunger pangs of girls working flat out. In the greenhouses the work was agreeable in the cold winter weather but was stifling in summer. The winter task of removing all the soil from the glasshouses and steam-sterilising was not undertaken by the landgirls but by those menfolk who had not been called up. The area covered by the LG estate was extensive with its boundary reaching the Little Pond, where the cluster of habitations there is known as Bogtrotters' Island.

For reasons not clear, landgirls were not allowed to use the NAAFI, but Churt's weekly dances provided welcome entertainment,

Gwynne's friendships formed during this period have lasted and she still keeps in touch with Nonie who now lives near Southend..

Alfred Wells

Alfred Wells standing on the crates of Cox's apples. 3,000 bushels were produced on the farm

Certain tuition for the land-girls fell to the lot of Alfred Wells, whose life was spent working on the land and whose clear reminiscences recall an era vastly altered during his lifetime. He was one of 8 sons and a daughter born to Frederick and Maud Wells and they all lived in a tiny cottage in Frensham. There were repeated problems over the tenancy of their cottage until at last his mother plucked up courage to visit the Great Man in Churt to ask his help. The long walk to Bron-y-de, pushing her youngest child in a pram, visibly exhausted her so that Mr Lloyd George's first instruction to his housekeeper was to offer tea and refreshments. As a result of the meeting, the Wells family some six months later moved into the first council house built at Peakfield, Frensham.

Alfred's working life started half an hour after he left school at 4pm on his 14th birthday. He worked for Mr Poulson of Frensham where his hours were from 5 am to 5.30 pm, 7 days a week. At the end of 5 years his wages rose to 18 shillings a week. After a short time working for Mr Thomas, whose private house eventually became Edgeborough School, Alfred took employment with Mr Combes of Pierrepont, an employer who cared for his staff. Tenants were permitted to make use of the land owned by him, taking sand for their own use and dead wood for fuel. Mr Combes forbade the new craze for motor biking on the Common, and also fined any motorists who attempted to park there on his land. He listened attentively as Alfred was brought before him for having caught a rabbit to take home to his wife and child. Recognising the difficulties of a young labourer in making ends meet, Mr Combes ordered that henceforth Alfred Wells was to receive a brace of fine rabbits each Saturday.

Harvest Home in the parish of Frensham

The death of Mr Combes in 1940 resulted in Alfred taking up work on the Lloyd George estate. He still recalls the anger among employees when, on the introduction of PAYE tax, their pay was made up for three days only, in order to simplify the work of the office staff. Alfred took the initiative in speaking directly with his employer about the suffering that would be caused to families as a result of this. Lloyd George righted the matter immediately.

Horsedrawn transport: Alfred Wells, left; Jim Voller, right

Staff took delight in hearing LG's down-to-earth sayings as he walked round his estate and remember his words 60 years later:

> *A woman, a dog and a walnut tree*
> *The more you thrash 'em*
> *The better they be.*

After the death of Earl Lloyd George, Alfred continued to work for the widowed Countess Lloyd George, who decided to have three fields brought into cultivation. Known as Faith, Hope and Charity, the fields proved to be hot, sandy and infertile so magnesium limestone was applied, then Welsh mountain oat seed was sown and undersown with grass and clover. The result was three good fields near Green Cross Farm.

Lady Lloyd George and her sister in the fruit orchards

Lady Lloyd George with her sister Muriel Stevenson examine the three reclaimed fields -
Faith, Hope and Charity, with their farm manager

Lloyd George's 80th birthday party. Alfred Wells is at the end of the table

Below, for the record, is yet another popular song about our most famous resident.

D'y ken Lloyd George with his coat so gay
He can shake it off and wear it either way
And deny tomorrow what he said today
And you'll wake with a head in the morning

D'y ken Lloyd George with his coat of gold
And the fairy tales which he oft times told
If you vote for him you'll be sadly sold
And you'll wake with a head in the morning

8: Recollections of a Nonagenarian Vicar

This account of life in the village in the 1950s is based on the recollections of the Rev. Hugh Seal and his wife Janet, 95 and 94 years, who are now living in Lancaster. Hugh was vicar of Churt from 1950-1957

In autumn 1950 the new vicar of Churt, Hugh Seal, together with his wife and 4-month-old baby, Judith, took up residence in the grand Victorian vicarage set in 3½ acres of garden. Their 10 year old son was away at school. Even before their arrival they had experienced the kindness of Churt when Lord Moreton and his mother Lady Aberdour invited them to spend a night or two with them at The Hatch saying simplicity was their lifestyle –"We don't change for dinner". He recalls his induction service when Admiral Sir William James recognised Hugh's brother with whom he'd worked at the Admiralty in 1936.

His first church service was bewilderingly deserted at 8 am, till he realised he'd failed to put his clock back the previous night. By the time of Hugh's arrival the choir had at long last received choristers' robes and, what's more, the girls were allowed to be seen.

The atmosphere of the village in the early '50s is described in Hugh's words: "It is not easy to explain to people of the present generation just how special those early post-World War II years were. Having lived through the stress and anxieties of the war years

The Old Vicarage in 1959. A view of the back of the house.

67

with their constant dangers, fears, privations and separations, it was as if the dark storm clouds had been scattered and sunshine had broken through. We could smile and laugh, we could hold our heads high and walk with a spring in our step. Although our arrival in Churt took place some five years after the end of hostilities this new sense of

The new vicarage nearing completion

peace and freedom was still in the air. The future was full of hope; life was good".

One particular characteristic of Churt struck the new vicar - it consisted of "plenty of bottom, plenty of top, but not much middle" though he was conscious there was a unity of purpose from all residents. This happy mix was to be found in church life. Judith their daughter was happy at the local school under the headship of Mr Basset, who also performed the duties of People's Churchwarden.

Bishop Montgomery Campbell at the blessing of the new vicarage in August 1954 with the Rev and Mrs Hugh Seal

Hugh recalls clearly so many persons and events: Mr Read the newsagent, Harold Martin the gardener at Sidlaws, Bert Voller the gravedigger, Admiral Sir William James and his wife Robin. Of the last pair he writes " Admiral James always read the lessons at Matins, very well too, but did not like my sermons to go on too long. After he had had enough he would ceremoniously take his fob watch from his waistcoat and give it a good looking-at – a signal to me to "round off" my homily".

Vice Admiral Nichol, General Akerman and Col. & Mrs Rose are warmly remembered, the last being "the family next door" at Old Kiln. It was the Roses who, on the day of the coronation in 1953, invited about a dozen people to their house to watch the ceremony on their television set with its 9 inch screen. At intervals their butler served tea and sandwiches.

Mr Bullock of Court Barn is remembered for his lovely garden and for becoming a "confirmand" at the age of 80. The ebullient Brough Ansdell at Quinnettes staged spectacular pageants and, on Guy Fawkes' Night, held a stupendous firework party to which the whole village was invited. Other names trip off the tongue after more than half a Century – Philip Brooks, Lady Lennard of Woodcote, the Bishops in Hale House Lane, the Lashes at Bridge End, Piers and Margaret Power at Follyfield, Lady Lloyd George, Col. Grazebrook of Jumps Road. This last was a Japanese prisoner-of-war and later became an ordained priest. Another notable family in the village were the Hunts of Hale House Farm, a Roman Catholic family who created a Catholic chapel from one of their farm outbuildings. "We possess in our archives a charming snap of our little daughter Judith receiving her Coronation Mug from Daphne Hunt, at the celebratory event held on the recreation ground".

The different shopkeepers are listed, including Mr Grimes who owned the garage managed by Mr Charman and from whom Hugh bought his first Ford car for £400.

The house, Silverbeck, is described as past the peak of its glory when the Seals arrived. "There, in her widowed splendour, lived Mrs Helen Goudie, a dour Scot, whose maiden name had been Walker (of whisky fame). She complained of "harrrd times – very harrrrd." At her funeral St John's Church was filled with her Scottish relatives and the Green was packed with Rolls-Royces parked nose to tail. The local paper discreetly noted her estate as £362,333.

The recreation ground was the site for the annual Flower Show. Mr Cooper, living at Redhearn, revitalised the tennis court when he offered free coaching to any youngster who came along. An active Youth Club was well supported by Nobby Novell, John Harris and Pam Eames.

It was during Hugh's incumbency that the old vicarage, antiquated, damp and with a leaking roof, was sold with 3 acres for £4,750 and a new one built in 1954 for £7,000. An area of land from the vicarage garden had been given in 1952 to enlarge the graveyard. Whilst the building was going on the Seals stayed at Gorse Cottage with Miss Ruth Hyde.

A final story still keenly fresh in Hugh's mind, is that of The Elusive Church Draughts and the involvement of Mr Peacock of Big Oak, an inveterate hoarder. Heating the church had been a long and continuing problem at St John's so when some of the congregation complained of draughts, particularly draughts associated with the organ, action was taken. One stormy winter's evening four men gathered in the church – the vicar, Admiral James, Mr Bishop (churchwarden), and Mr M'Guire the organist - and

The Rev Hugh Seal and his wife Janet in 2003, aged 94 and 93

they were met by super-efficient Mr Peacock who had brought candles, boxes of matches, and cards on which to put the dripping candles. On hands and knees they examined every inch of the church, seeking a tell-tale flicker from the flame. After a while they noticed that the cards catching the wax drips had been something special; they were at least 40 years old, invitations from Queen Alexandra to some London function, all in perfect condition. The wind howled. Mr M'Guire played the organ, said by some to be the source of the trouble. "Louder, M'Guire, Louder!" roared the Admiral and the organ bellowed forth. The candles did not respond. After a while, chilled to the bone, the stalwarts filed out, with nothing to report to the Parochial Church Council.

After spending seven years at the Church of St John the Evangelist, Churt, Hugh and his family moved to a coalmining parish in the North with a population of 24,000. Since his retirement in 1979, he and his family have revisited Churt and met several old friends. They are a remarkable couple who keep up a copious correspondence with friends old and new.

A selection of covers of Church Magazines Over the Years

April 1917

June 1925

Churt Parish Magazine

No. 1   JANUARY, 1944.

Vicar and Surrogate (for issuing Marriage Licences): Rev. B. H. Bosanquet, M.A. (Tel. Headley Down 3253).
Churchwardens: Major-General W. P. Akerman, C.B., D.S.O., M.C., and Mr. P. T. Browne.
Organist and Choirmaster: Mr. G. Hastings.
Hon. Treasurer (to whom all subscriptions should be sent): Mr. W. H. R. Peacock, Big Oak, Churt. (Tel. Headley Down 3163).
Hon. Secretary, P.C.C.: Mr. H. E. Bishop, Foresters, Churt. (Tel. Headley Down 3210).
District Nurse: Nurse Matthewson, Oeanay, Recreation Ground, Churt. (Tel. Headley Down 3167).

CHURCH SERVICES.

Parish Church.

SUNDAYS.—Holy Communion, 8 a.m. (Third Sunday 11 a.m.); Great Festivals : 7 a.m., 8 a.m., noon. Saints' Days : As announced. Matins : 11 a.m. Evensong, 6.30 p.m. (Summer), 3.30 (Winter). Holy Baptism : At Evensong or by arrangement. Churchings by arrangement.

Tilford Road Mission.

Lay Reader: Mr. T. W. Bridge.

Holy Communion : Second Sunday, 10 a.m., and as announced. Service : Sundays, 6.30 p.m. (Summer), 3 p.m. (Winter).
Church Lending Library: Open in Vestry First Friday in the month, 2.30 to 3.30 p.m.

Notes.—The Vicar may generally be found at home on Weekdays (except Saturdays), between 2 p.m. and 2.30 p.m., 5 p.m. and 5.30 p.m., and after 8 p.m.

Not less than three days' notice should be given of Banns of Marriage.

NOTICES FOR THE MONTH.

January, 1944.

Sundays: Holy Communion, 8.30 a.m., and on [...] a.m.

Saturday, January 1st: The Circumcision. New Y[...] 10.30 a.m.

January 1944 during the wartime paper shortage

January 1952

CHURT PARISH MAGAZINE

JANUARY, 1952.   No. 1

Parish Church of St. John the Evangelist.

CHURCH SERVICES

Sundays :
  Holy Communion : 8.0 a.m.
    First Sunday : 9.15 a.m.
    Third Sunday : 9.15 a.m. and 11 a.m.
  Matins : 11.0 a.m.
  Evensong : 6.30 p.m.
  Sunday School : 2.30 p.m.
Wednesdays :
  Holy Communion : 11.0 a.m.
Matins and Evensong are said daily at 7.30 a.m. and 6 p.m., except Tuesdays and as announced.
Holy Baptism and Churching by arrangement.
Saints' Days :
  Holy Communion : 8 a.m.

Tilford Road Church Room

Sundays :
  Holy Communion : Second Sunday, 9.15 a.m.
  Evensong : 3.45 p.m. (every Sunday).
  Sunday School : 3.45 p.m.
Thursdays :
  Holy Communion : 8 a.m.

Langham, Printers, Farnham.

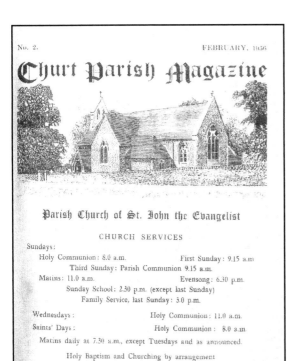

November 2003

Uncovered recently in the garden of the Old Vicarage was this memorial to a favourite pet: "Michael. 1910 - 1928 To some a Persian Cat. To us, just Michael." The Rev B H Bosanquet was vicar from 1925 to 1946.

9: Frensham Common and Aviation

Frensham Common and the Great Pond, August 2002

Frensham Common lies mostly in the Parish of Frensham but it is an essential part of life in Churt, providing opportunities for riding, walking and picnicking as well as the study of the rare flora and fauna on the world-renowned heathland.

But this area has interesting associations with aviation, as well as with the more familiar military camp sites. Ramblers on the Common have observed three monuments. Two, near Kettlebury Hill, commemorate a tragic air accident in 1932. One flat stone is clearly marked Emily Bossom fell here July 27 1932. A second similar stone has the name Bruce Bossom inscribed on it.

A third monument relates to two brothers killed in the First World War.

The 1930s accident, involving a Puss Moth aircraft, is still recalled by several people and, of course, there is the Air Ministry Official Report on Accident Investigations into Puss Moths (No. 1699) . The plane G-ABDH which crashed at Churt shortly after 1800 hours on 27th July 1932 during an alarming

Memorial stones to Emily Bayne Bossom and her son Bruce

summer lightning storm was piloted by Bruce Bossom aged 21. He and his two passengers were all killed - his mother, Emily Bayne Bossom, wife of Alfred C Bossom, Conservative MP for Maidstone, and Count Otho Erbach-Fursternau (23) a family friend. The plane was on its way to Southampton from Heston. As it disappeared into the storm a rending noise was heard and a few seconds later the machine was seen to fall in pieces from out of the sky. A major inquiry was initiated on nine accidents to Puss Moths which showed structural problems with these aircraft. The inquest was held at the Court House, Farnham. Shortly afterwards a reward was offered for a string of black pearls lost in the crash. In her time off work at the vicarage Ruth Croucher was one of the searchers but eventually the necklace was found by a man from Thursley. It is not known when the two memorial stones were placed on the Common.

Puss Moth photo: Bill Houghton

The third monument, one of several in the south-east, relates not to fliers but to two brothers killed in the First World War. The obelisk faces the road and overlooks the Great Pond. On the side is a plaque which reads: "Frensham Common was bequeathed to the National Trust by W A Robertson in memory of his brothers Norman Cairns Robertson, Captain 2nd Battalion Hampshire Regiment who died 20.6.1916 at Hanover, Germany, and of Laurence Grant Robertson, 2nd Lieutenant Battalion King's Own Scottish Borderers, killed in action in France during the Battle of the Somme in or near Selville Wood, 13.1.1916". The two named on the plaque were the younger pair

The obelisk at Highcomb Copse

of four brothers. The War Graves Commission states that Capt. N C Roberstson is buried in Hamburg; he was aged 40 and was the son of William and Mary Robertson of 24 Cranley Gardens, London SW10. Second Lt. L G Robertson has no known grave and is commemorated on the Thiepval memorial in France. He was 36.

Detail from the obelisk at Highcomb Copse

In 1937 the eldest brother, W A Robertson, died and left the whole of his money on trust to the National Trust to erect a number of these monuments with almost the same wording. Hence they are to be found not only at Frensham Common but at Sutton House, Hackney, Robertson Corner on the top of Dunstable Down in Bedfordshire, Toys Hill, Sevenoaks area of Kent, Micheldean near Beachy Head, Sharpenhoe Clappers also in Bedfordshire, some 15 miles from the Dunstable Down memorial, Hydon's Ball, Milford, Netley

Detail from the obelisk at
Highcomb Copse

Park near Shere and Highcomb Copse, Hindhead.

Frensham Common has come into the hands of the National Trust from various donations of land at different times. In 1924 266 hectares of land including the Great Pond and some cottages were bought by public subscription and given to the National Trust. In the same year 14 hectares at Stoney Jump were donated, largely due to the generosity of Frank Mason of Churt. The gift by the W A Robertson Trust consisted of 266 hectares in 1940. Further land given in 1945 included the Flashes, whilst in 1970 Hambledon Rural District Council gave 3.6 hectares to include the remaining stretch of the Great Pond. The most recent donation occurred in 1974 when F S D Atherton gave cottages, a boathouse and nature reserve near the Little Pond.

This large area of commonland, with far fewer trees than at present, had always been a great attraction to aviators. More than a Century ago, in 1880, ballooning came to Frensham Common for, after James Sadler ascended in a hydrogen-filled balloon in 1785 at Molesey in Surrey, the army realised its military potential, particularly for use as an observation platform to view enemy movements. Thus the Royal Engineers formed the first balloon unit in 1878 and in 1880 the aeronauts camped at Frensham Pond after their manoeuvres at Aldershot. Their ascent attracted hundreds of fascinated spectators. It is interesting to note that an area to the east of the Great Pond, where these 1880 manoeuvres were observed is, in the 21st Century, now a

A military balloon operated by the Royal Engineers at Frensham Great Pond. 1880

military area of restricted access to civilian planes.

The first seaplane being tried on Frensham Great Pond, 1913

Aldershot and Farnborough provided a focus for development of flying and in 1913 the Great Pond became the site of the first seaplane trials. The RE1 reconnaissance tractor biplane was later fitted with floats and known as the HRE. This was tested on Fleet and Frensham Ponds by Geoffrey de Havilland. The plane was brought by road from Farnborough where it had been built and underwent her first tests successfully.

The area's long association with aviation was continued in World War II when pilots made the present Pond Hotel their local pub.

Eventually private individuals took to the air in their own aircraft and the village of Churt has its own airstrip lying to the west of the ponds in a slight hollow. The 1 km-long grass runway faces east-west to avail itself of the prevailing wind. On a summer's evening, reports one of the few pilots using the site, it is idyllic, perfectly still, save for the singing of numerous skylarks, A decade ago the East Hampshire District Council authorised it as an accepted airstrip but severely restricted the number of take-offs and landings.

The crew of the unofficial winner of the London-Sydney air race - Mike Miller, James D'Arcy, Mark Graham and John D'Arcy - celebrate landing in Australia yesterday. Thirty-eight planes from ten countries set out from London on March 11 to complete the 14,000-mile journey, sponsored by the Australian government, to recreate the race of 1919. (Sunday Times 8 April 2001)

In 2001 international success came to two of the Churt pilots. The Australian Government sponsored a competition re-creating the 1919 air race from London to Sydney. It was won by John D'Arcy and son James, pilots from Churt aerodrome, and their crew.

At a time when the British public takes to the air in droves, it is amusing to read an excerpt from a letter to The Times written in 1909 by Major B Baden-Powell:

It has clearly been demonstrated that apparatus can now be made which can carry men through the air in a practical manner, and there seems to be every probability that within the next few years many machines will be constructed capable of travelling hundreds of miles through the air, swiftly, surely and safely.

He goes on to ask whether *"these air-hogs are to be allowed to pass over our private property, gliding over our chimney-pots or skim close above our lawns and flower-beds?"* and recommended urgent international legislation.

10: Music Making in Churt

Churt's interest in music is evident but there are few written records relating to music in the village. We hear of bands being formed, choirs competing, concerts in Big Houses, folk-songs being preserved, innumerable village concerts taking place which included singing and playing instruments, but reports are scrappy. It is best to start with the church.

The original 1838, unconsecrated, church had a gallery where traditionally the musicians sat playing such instruments as the violin, viol, serpent, bassoon and flute, so that the congregation literally turned to face the music. (We have no record of what instruments our players used). However, in 1883 the gallery was removed during alterations . There are later indications that only the choir was responsible for the singing, not the congregation. Mr Watson, vicar from

A Serpent

1884 to 1917, started our monthly magazine and in 1892 he was delighted to record that the choir wore surplices for the first time. Mr Rose, Headmaster at the school, besides being the choir master was also the founder of the Fife and Drum Band, known as the Institute Band. In announcing the forthcoming Christmas arrangements the vicar remarked in 1894 that "Some carols will *probably* be sung at the Christmas Day Services." The choir were provided with new hymn books in 1899. Though 'Hymns Ancient and Modern', first published in 1861, was meant to introduce communal singing, it seems not to have appealed to our congregations for in 1918 Mr Barton, the vicar, pronounced "The singing of a country church should be *congregational.* We hope that the congregation will take their full share in every part of the service."

In an attempt to encourage church singing the first Ruridecanal Choir Festival took place at Farnham Church on Wednesday June 3rd 1896 when nearly every choir in the Deanery took part, including Churt. At this time, of course, there were no women singers, so how did the men get time off work? Later, women sang, but were hidden. Pam Eames, who joined the choir in 1947 at the age of 13, spoke of the time when girls and women were finally allowed to be seen in the choir stalls.

Local military bands played at Churt's Flower Shows and often at school concerts. At a time when all entertainment had to be home produced there were often full houses at events put on in the schoolroom. The school was proud to offer "Nigger Songs" in 1895.

Meanwhile the children were taught songs at school, rousing patriotic songs which were sung on Empire Day 1909: Here's a health unto his Majesty, Up with the Old Flag, Rule Britannia, Land of Hope and Glory and, of course, the National Anthem. Music is very much part of St John's School's curriculum in the 21st Century, with recorder tuition and lively singing in their annual Christmas production.

About 1906 a Churt Choral Society was formed with an annual subscription of 2s 6d. Miss Chesney was its first conductor followed in 1907 by Mr Allen of Spreakley. They experienced the magic of a gramophone in 1911 when Mr Bryan Hook of Silverbeck demonstrated his at the choir's annual supper.

Meanwhile a national movement affected Churt, when collectors of old folk-songs visited the village and found rich pickings.

"Singing was one of life's free pleasures" maintained the traditional labourer. "You would often hear a man singing at his work. A man would sing out unabashed as he strode through the village." Such a man must have been Jesse Voller of Churt, for when Cecil Sharp began a movement in 1903 to record England's folk-songs before they disappeared he prompted others to do the same. Thus, in 1912 and 1913, Clive Carey visited Churt and wrote down the songs he heard being sung by Jesse Voller and Andrew Dobson.

Neither Sharp nor Carey was the first serious collector of English folk-songs. That role fell to the Reverend S Baring-Gold, remembered in this area for his novel "The Broomsquire", but known throughout the church for his hymns 'Onward Christian soldiers' and 'Now the Day is Over'. Baring-Gold had published his first collection of Devonshire songs and tunes in 1889.

Jesse Voller was a farm labourer working at Green Cross Farm on 7th October 1913 when Carey recorded 'Broom, Green Broom' with its rollicking tune. Described as an amoral song, for idleness is rewarded with the hand of a rich and lovely lady, it starts:

> *There was an old man, who lived in the west*
> *His trade it was cutting of broom, green broom.*
> *And he had a lazy boy, Jack, for his son*
> *Who lay in his bed till 'twas noon, high noon.*
> *Who lay in his bed till 'twas noon*

Then when the lady, attracted by the scamp's good looks and lusty voice, asks

> *Honest blade, will you give up your trade*
> *And marry a lady in bloom?*

We are pleased to learn

> *Then Jack gave consent, and to the church went,*
> *He married her there in the room.*
> *Now they live at their ease, and they kiss when they please,*
> *That's better than crying of broom, green broom,!*
> *That's better than crying of broom!*

Well done, broomsquire!

The Broomsquire

So many of the lyrics tell of partings, betrayed love and death. Each song has many verses; the memories of the singers must have been prodigious. We have copies of the 13 lyrics and tunes passed on by Jesse, and the same for 6 from Andrew.

There are several indications in the 1930s of an increasing musical interest in the village. The well-known Dr L P Hutchings gave an organ recital in the church on New Year's Day, 1933. Music was performed in the Big houses, several of which possessed a Music Room. Their owners invited a chosen audience to listen to famous artists such as Sir John Barbirolli, Sir Benjamin Britten, Yehudi Menuhin and Peter Pears (himself born in Farnham.) One such house was Pine House, then home of the Gill family, where the Hindhead and Haslemere Music Society met frequently and considered Pine House to be the home of their concerts until 1975, Nellie Gill having died in 1970. Country Life of 20th September 1936 has an article on the construction of the music room where the floor is of a special mastic composition to assist acoustics.

Conductor Jane Beattie with the rose bowl won by Frensham Ladies' Choir as the best all-round choir at Petersfield Festival. Holding the other two cups won in the same competition are (right) former conductor Margaret Power and one of the choir's soloists, Aileen Pearson

Another venue for concerts was Woodcote, home of Lady Lennard in the 1950s. Lady Lennard's sister, a talented pianist, lived in nearby Tyndrum and arranged these concerts. Before Mr & Mrs Frank Martin moved into Woodcote they attended the last of Lady Lennard's concerts and were introduced to the audience as the new owners who might be persuaded to carry on the tradition of music in the house. This Frank promptly did by joining the Festival Singers, a mixed choral society, becoming its conductor and competing in the Aldershot Festival where, for three years running, they won the cup and a banner.

The thriving Churt Youth Club in the 1950s and 60s had an enthusiastic choir section which gave performances in the church and village hall.

1996, The Chase Singers gathered for a concert at Quinnettes. Those in the picture include Milva Sandison (conductor), Lindi Kornblum (director of St Joseph's Centre at Haslemere Hospital, for which the concert was in aid), Victoria Davies (harpist), Janet Burton, Jane Hamlyn, Mary Donald, Monica Macready, Jean Kirk, Sarah Bourne, Brigid Tucker, Pam Jessop, Katherine Thomas, Joan Clary, Lesley Field, Ann Rawlinson, Diana Harding, Betty Penney, Mary Grocott, Elizabeth Bagnall, Susie Briars.

The WI has proved a fertile source of female voices. Prior to the founding of a WI in Churt in 1919, Margaret Power had started a choir of a dozen or so voices. This choir became the core of the WI Ladies Choir led by Margaret and, as it had a majority of Frensham WI members, was known as Frensham WI Choir. The Frensham members kindly paid for practices at the Merindin Hall but, with increasing support from Churt members, the choir changed its name to Frensham and Churt Choir, both WIs contributing to the hiring costs. They had repeated successes at a number of Music Festivals. By the

1960s when Jane Beattie became its leader it was totally independent of Frensham. The Churt Ladies Choir met at Chase House and became known as "The Chase Singers". Appropriately its next conductor, Milva Sandison, lived at Chase House. The Chase Singers are now well-known throughout the district. Valerie Hoppe (in 2004 awarded MBE for her services to music) led the choir when Milva was absent. Now the eagerly awaited concerts are again led by Milva, memorably in Farnham Castle.

1986: Over 60s Choir at a Christmas celebration.
From left to right: Margaret Power (conductor), Melene Barnes,
Phyllis Lillywhite, Geoffrey Bayston (partly obscured), Primrose Thomas, Marian Jenkins,
Joyce Chuter, "Lucky", (two obscured),
Marjorie Eales

Meanwhile the Over 60s Club formed its own choir which gained several trophies in local competitions under its conductor Margaret Power, who was still highly active with them in her 80s.

Over 60s Choir, in the 1980s

A professional instrument maker, Christopher Monk, created the almost obsolete instrument, the serpent, at his home at Churt in the 1970s. Another former Churt resident, Vincent Lindsey Clark, has become an acclaimed professional guitarist.

Carol singing round the village continued for many years with mince pies, coffee and more stimulating drinks being an added inducement offered by householders.

We have been fortunate in having music lovers among our vicars. The Rev. Hugh Seal MA, LRAM, and his wife Janet performed at a concert in Churt Village Hall on April 10th and 11th (year unspecified in the programme), Hugh on violin, Janet on cello and with May Kirkland accompanying them on piano. Well into their 90s they still perform chamber concerts at home with their friends in Lancaster. The Rev. Stuart Thomas had reached concert standard as a pianist and still gives concert recitals, though he left Churt in 1994. Our present Resident Minister, Sophie Jelley, is a viola player and singer.

Undoubtedly, there must be many more accounts of music-making in Churt waiting to be discovered.

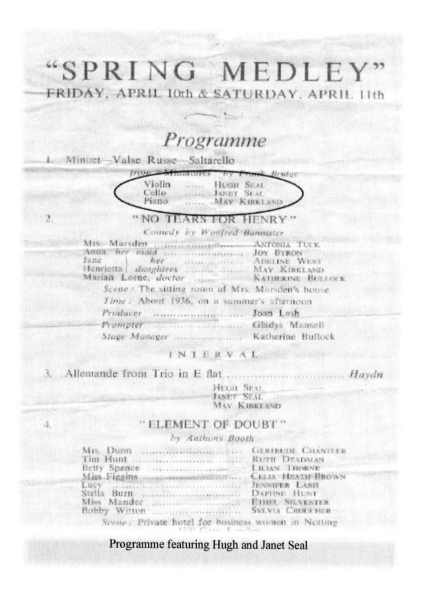

Programme featuring Hugh and Janet Seal

11: Hale House, a Pictorial History

Hale House

One of Churt's interesting old houses is Hale House, still a farm in the early 1950s. It is from our various Mediaevalists that its history can be traced. Even the definition of Hale is uncertain; some say it means "a small corner of land"; others say it means "a lodging in the wasteland". There is fairly reliable evidence that the land associated with the house was cleared in the 13th Century. What is certain is that when William Bristowe acquired Hale House and its land in late 1572 he pulled down almost all the 15th Century house, retaining one bay in the new structure. He stipulated that on his death, whilst his daughter Rebecca inherited the farm, nevertheless his widow was to keep the "lower room called the cupperd chamber standing westward" and was to have access to the chimney and fire and be free to do her baking. She was also to have £10 per annum. By 1746 Dr George Holme, rector of Headley, was in possession of Hale House Farm and he presented it to Queen's College, Oxford, in trust for contributions to the charity school at Headley and for grants to four scholars at Queen's. For a period Hale House Farm was known as College Farm. Later it reverted to its former name, Hale House Farm.

Hale House Farm in the early 20ᵗʰ Century

The Domestic Buildings Research Group, in its report on the property, stated "The house incorporates remnants of an old open hall building with a later crosswing added by the Bristowes". When Major Hunt bought Hale House in the 1950s, it was a working farm.

Hale House in the 1950s

The owners prior to Major Hunt had created gardens which, over the next 53 years, were tended by Norman Bone (pictured right), still gardening at Hale House though well into his 80s.

Norman Bone

The farm kitchen with its Belfast sink

In this early aerial view (above) the barn in front of the vegetable patch was converted by the Hunt family into a Roman Catholic chapel with a bell on the gable to summon worshippers and an entrance from the back gate.

It was part of the gardener's duties to prepare the chapel with flowers before the service.

Major Hunt suffered from Parkinson's disease and his wife resided next door in Fircone Cottage. His son John, Sir John, later Lord Hunt, lived at Hale House but eventually moved to Wimble-don. In succession, the owners of

The Roman Catholic chapel in the barn

Hale House since then have been the Ordes, the Scotts, the Beckers, the Kents and now Mr & Mrs Kilpatrick. To all these owners Norman has served as gardener helping to maintain a garden whose herbaceous border especially is famed among garden lovers.

Mrs Kilpatrick with Norman Bone in 2004

Norman Bone at work

12: Old Churt and an Old Property, Hyde Farm

An earlier sketch of Hyde Farm originating in the 14th Century

The Churt we live in today has existed for centuries not, of course, as we now know it. Little fragments of population lived in small patches of land which have since joined into one whole village. The gardens we tend today were walked upon by earlier inhabitants as they cultivated their fields, each field having a name which is recorded on the 1839 Tithe map.

Archivists such as Pat Heather, Mark Page, Greta Turner, as well as the late Philip Brooks and Elfrida Manning, have delved into Churt's Mediaeval past. Here, we take a brief glimpse at this earlier period.

Let us begin with a gentle reminder of the antiquity of Churt.

Anne's Cottage/Shiloh/The Toft: (default of rent) 1292

Cherry Tree Cottage 1745

Green Farm started around... 1338

Greencroft/ Collyn's Croft Cottage, on site since............................ 1348

Greencross Farm. Site cleared in 13C, bought from Wm le Wayte.......... 1352

Hale House: difficult to date its beginnings, definite references 1572

Marchants; existed with no Mediaeval name; first recorded tenant was..... 1320

Moorside.. 1341

Old Barn Cottage/ Warryners occupied by Bishop's "rabbit-keepers"...... 1489

Outmoor/Andrews: occupation started early 13C. Area was extended..... 1244

Old Forge: uncertain; it has definite references in 1516

Old Post Office: on edge of common, believed to have been there since.. 16th Century

Quinnettes: difficult, long-occupied; certain definite references in 1550

Ridgeway Farm/Childewell or Zeld. A house existed there in................ 1317

Stock Farm – land cleared.. 1451

Hyde Farm, one of Churt's very old properties, is the subject of this section.

The very earliest date ascribed to the tract of land known as "Hyde" is 688. Brooks believed that a bank on its eastern boundary was not only the eastern border of Churt, but that it probably delineated an outer limit of the two hides of land given to the church by Caedwalla in 688. Unfortunately, the bank was flattened in 1940.

An interior view

The Winchester Pipe Rolls, which record the dues received by the Bishop of Winchester from the 13th to 17th centuries, include many references to Hyde. Before surnames became necessary we read that Richard atte Hide was working the land in 1211 and William atte Hide in 1244.

Another interior view

In 1348 the Black Death arrived in England decimating the population, Churt not excepted. The result was that many rents remained unpaid, the land was neglected. The people at Hyde were sorely affected for the records show that in 1349 and 1350 Roger atte Hide paid no rent. It took Churt nearly 150 years to recover its numbers after the devastation of the Plague. When records resume, after a Century's silence, they tell of an enterprising individual Thomas Luffe who, as a copyholder, bought a number of smallholdings on the eastern side of Churt which were without tenants. These were amalgamated into one farm which became known as Hyde Farm, and so once again the bishop received his rent.

The Luffe family continued to live at Hyde from 1503-1700s, but not in the same house because, at the end of the 16th Century, a certain John Luffe had the old house taken down and a new one built. He kept the old kitchen block and built on to it a house with a chimney and an oriel window on the east. After Thomas Luffe died in 1761 the property then descended through the female line and the name Poulton was introduced. The name Poulton continues and Minchin and Baker relate a story about George Poulton (died 1797), a prosperous but sporting yeoman of Hyde Farm, whose yearly custom was to drive a four-in-hand to the Derby. On one return he missed his way and steered his coach into the spring pond. Thereafter, this event is repeated in ghostly fashion the night after the Derby has been run.

Hyde Farm 1921 as owned by Lord Ashcombe

Hyde farm and its owners are indirectly connected with Churt's church, for it was in 1838 that Henry Wheeler of Binsted, associated by marriage with Hyde, gave some of his waste land in Churt for the building of the Church.of St John the Evangelist.

The farm in 1973 when Peter and Felicity Miller bought it.

By the early 20th Century Lord Ashcombe was the owner of Hyde Farm as part of the 2,035 acre Cubitt Estate he held in Churt. His estate was auctioned in 1921 and from the auction particulars we see that his tenant at Hyde Farm from 1915 was Mr A W Andrews, paying £53 10s 0d annual rent for some 59 acres. "Country Life" featured the farm in an article of about 1921.

The barn built by Peter and Felicity Miller.

The following is a description of the house by the Domestic Buildings Research Group in the late 20th Century: . *The present house Hyde Farm is a fine timber-framed building dating from several periods, the oldest surviving part being of the 15th Century, originally a 2-bay building which was used as a kitchen to a separate house. The large barn on the farmstead was demolished in the early 20th Century.*

Now, in the 21st Century, Hyde Farm is one of Churt's oldest and most delightful properties as the photographs show. Peter & Felicity Miller were farming Hyde in the 1970s in conjunction with Stanley Billiald of Hyde Cottage. They bought in calves and over two years fattened them before selling them for slaughter or for store cattle. They put up new barns and used the latest feeding methods. In addition, Felicity bred some registered Connemara Ponies.

May Hyde long continue to have diligent owners.

13: 2004 - Centenary Year for Hindhead Golf Club

For many years West Surrey was taboo – a desert, fit only for army exercises. Gradually it found itself as "the lung of London" and Hindhead developed as a desirable holiday resort with palatial guest houses. New residences were erected there and at Grayshott and Haslemere so that in late Victorian times Hindhead and its neighbouring villages held a "small aristocracy of artists". Quite naturally the thoughts of these new residents turned to golf and where to play. The result was the 9-hole Hankley Golf Course which opened in 1896 with Churt's vicar, Rev. A W Watson, as a founder member and Captain from 1896-7.

A few years later a meeting of "carriage folk" took place in Tower Road, Hindhead, to discuss the possibility of another golf course. The area selected was the open, windy, barren moorland of Hindhead with its 6 radiating hollows called Bottoms: Heccombe (Punch Bowl); Pit Fall Bottom (Nutcombe Valley); Stoney Bottom; Whitmoor Bottom (Whitmoor Vale); Woodcock Bottom

(Golden Valley) and Poor Devil's Bottom (4th& 5th holes of the Golf Club). The area required for an 18-hole course was 150 acres, of which 110 were leased from the Hon H S Cubitt and the remainder from James Mayhew a yeoman farmer. At an altitude of 649 feet there were views of Frensham Ponds and the southern slopes of the North Downs from the Hog's Back to the cornfields above Alton. Herons flew over regularly on their route from the heronry at Crosswater to Waggoners Wells. The club opened in April 1904. Mr A J Whitaker, Squire of Grayshott, was the first Captain and the first full Golf Club Committee included Mr C E C Prichard of Llanover, Churt.

Three years later after heavy snow the President, Sir ArthurConan Doyle, skied down from his house Undershaw (on the present A3) down the Churt Road into the clubhouse and then over to Poor Devil's Bottom and the 18th green.

The first decade of the 20th Century saw an increase in motorised traffic, which extended the average 15 mile radius of the Victorian carriage. George Bernard Shaw who lived locally complained that the Hindhead Hills were being invaded by an "80 horse-power weekend bridge-playing lot". The LSWR train service tried to compete with the motorcar by increasing its frequency from Waterloo and offering cheap day-return tickets for members.

In 1910 the leasehold arrangements were revised when Cubitt offered to sell 130 acres at £100 per acre but the club was unable to raise that sum. (At a later date he offered Lloyd George 60 acres at £60 per acre.) Eleven years later members were to be astonished to read an advertisement saying the Cubitt Estate was being auctioned including " a major portion of the Hindhead Golf Links". The Secretary, Mr E Turle, negotiated a settlement.

Both wars affected the club. In World War I troops were billeted in the clubhouse at 9 pence per head per night. Agricultural interests eyed the golf links when Surrey County Council asked firstly, if farmers could graze their sheep on the course and secondly, in 1917, whether the course could be ploughed up. Both possibilities were averted. In World War II all the Surrey Golf clubs were called to Whitehall, and Hindhead was again asked if its course could be used for food production. Again it was deemed unsuitable. When the British and Canadian armies had petrol "for recreational purposes", golfing flourished.

In 1944 a Dornier 217 hit the crest of the hill above Whitmore Vale, 50 yards from the 17th tee just missing the clubhouse. The crew of four was killed.

In 1919 the club's exclusiveness was reduced by a degree of liberalisation when artisans, to a maximum number of 50, from Hindhead and Churt, but not Grayshott, were allowed to play under the new "Hindhead and Churt Village Club" before 9 am and after 3 pm. The last rounds under this scheme were played in 1965.

Churt continued to provide members. Two, Mr H McNaughton of Rosemead and Mr K Treherne-Thomas, sometimes travelled uphill by bus. As Mr McNaughton weighed 23 stones the conductor never allowed them to sit together behind the back axle. When Harry McNaughton was alone, the bus was lopsided as far as the clubhouse . In 1919 Mr Frank Mason of Churt, later to become the donor of Churt's village hall, was made Captain. David Lloyd George was made an honorary Life Member of the club 6 weeks before his resignation as Prime Minister on 19th December 1922.

In 1946 land was bought on mortgage from Lord Ashcombe (formerly Cubitt) and the substantial mortgage was transferred to a member, Mr R C Bett (described as hugely rich), on the basis that it would be paid off in his will and accordingly the remaining £4,358 was settled. By 1950 Admiral Sir William James of Churt was President and his term of office included several financial problems. A new constitution in 1970 superseded the original almost unaltered since the time of Sir Arthur Conan Doyle and Whitaker. The clubhouse was rebuilt in 1977.

A history of the Club is currently in preparation.

14: Jumps House, a Victorian Melodrama

Contributed by William Tate

Originally called The Observatory when built in 1866 by its first owner, the famous Victorian astronomer Richard Carrington (1826 – 1875), Jumps House has an absorbing story to tell. The 'goings on' there are worthy of any tabloid newspaper – love, prostitution, jealousy, intrigue, assault, mysterious deaths, accusations of murder and suicide, a lunatic asylum and ghosts. Copies of the newspapers of the time graphically regaled the incredulous public with news of the scandals which emerged at the trial of an assailant in 1871 and at the inquests of Carrington's wife, Rose, in 1875 and his own shortly thereafter.

Richard Christopher Carrington, Fellow of the Royal Society, was already famous as an astronomer when he moved from his observatory at Redhill to Churt. He acquired 19 acres of land in 1857 in order to construct a second observatory, this one atop the central of three strange conical hills: High Jump, Middle Jump and Stoney Jump. These 'jumps' border the area known as The Flashes and are formed of an unusual type of iron sandstone. They are called 'jumps' because, in legend, the Devil jumped from one to another before leaping into the Devil's Punchbowl at Hindhead.

Carrington tunnelled into Middle Jump, down from the top and sideways from ground level, so that scientific equipment could be located deep underground at a constant temperature, to assist his research into sun spots, which he pioneered.

He built his house – described then as a 'large, luxurious mansion' with six bedrooms, all on the ground floor – at the base of Middle Jump in what was then a substantial estate with 'a dairy, large fowl houses, dog kennels, piggery and cowshed' and 'a coach house and stalls for two horses, groom's cottage etc'. There was also a small building on top of nearby High Jump for 'painting cloudscapes'.

Some pictorial evidence of Jumps House and the observatory exists from *The Illustrated London News* of 16 September 1871 when Lieutenant S. P. Oliver, R.A., encamped on The Flashes with the 3rd Division in the Autumn Campaign, made a sketch of the three Jumps viewed from near the apex of Stoney Jump. The land was then more open heathland, with views less hindered by today's heavily wooded landscape. The magazine's etching shows a building much larger than today's.

Jumps House now stands in 5 acres of woodland, the remaining acreage sold off long ago. And the house itself is now a modest affair, most of the rooms having been demolished in attempts to drive away ghosts. A crude comparison can be made by comparing the Ordinance Survey maps of the area between 1871 and 1895.

Etching made from a sketch of the Jumps by Lieutenant S. P. Oliver, R.A.
(*The Illustrated London News*, 16 September 1871)

The rooms that survived the cull were assigned the role of mere 'gardener's cottage', until extensions were added to the small Victorian core around 1940. But whose ghosts, and what led to the mysterious deaths?

Partially demolished Jumps House reduced to a gardener's cottage, 1928

In a tale reminiscent of Professor Henry Higgins' infatuation with Eliza Doolittle in George Bernard Shaw's *Pygmalian*, Richard Carrington fell for a London prostitute, Rose, whom he met in Regent Street. "Tall and perfectly formed, with an exquisite face, the sweetest expression, and possessing a manner whose charm and fascination was instantly overwhelming", the beautiful Rose became his wife in 1869 and they moved in to Jumps House.

But when the astronomer was in London at meetings of the Royal Astronomical Society, the youthful Rose, then aged around 25, continued a long-standing liaison with a 52-years-old former trooper in the 4th Dragoon Guards named William Rodway. Richard Carrington knew of Rodway, but Rose had told him that he was her brother. Curiously, on her marriage certificate to Carrington, Rose's surname is given as Jeffries, but she is reported to have first told Carrington her name was Rodway. There was speculation that she might have been married to William Rodway at some time.

Rodway and Rose had resided together in Putney, living in some style off her immoral earnings. On leaving the Army, Rodway had become a ring master with General Tom Thumb and Howe's American circus. Rose accompanied him on tours around the country. They remained close. Even on the morning of her wedding to Carrington, Rose and Rodway breakfasted together. She also went to stay with him for a few days on her return from honeymoon in Paris, before she settled into a comfortable relationship with her new husband for a couple of years. But even then, when Rose travelled to London, she would be met by Rodway at Waterloo station and they would go to a private hotel in the Waterloo Road for a couple of hours.

William Rodway had a strong hold over Rose and, after her marriage to Carrington, he frequently called on her at The Observatory to demand money that she had acquired from Carrington. On 18 August 1871, in an argument witnessed by the cook concerning Mr Carrington's pet dog which Rodway was trying to drag away from Rose, the couple struggled in the front hall and Rodway stabbed Rose with a new 5-inch blade clasp knife. He then inflicted seven wounds to his own chest. Both Rose and Rodway bled profusely, but both survived. Rose called for the servants. One came but did not say a word or move a finger to help her mistress. Why? Apart from Rose's low morals, it was speculated that the maid possibly despised her as an illiterate who couldn't even write her own name, and who lacked the bearing to command servants.

Rose ran to the nearby Devil's Jumps Inn (now The Cedars, a private residence in Jumps Road), and received aid. At his trial at Farnham Court an incomplete blood-stained letter written by Rodway was produced by the prosecution as evidence of attempted murder: "I have stabbed the woman to the heart, I hope …". But the defence argued that Rodway would have intended to complete the letter "… I hope either for her recovery or my death." Rodway's confession stated "I've done all there is to be done, and if I've injured her I am sorry for it. I resolved to kill myself before her eyes". But the jury disbelieved Rodway and his defence. Before the incident Rodway had been heard boasting that Carrington would not keep her for much longer: "Before a month is over I'll have her dead or alive". Accordingly, Rodway was convicted of assault with intent to murder and sent to prison for 20 years' penal servitude at Knaphill, Woking, where he died just a few years later in 1874. Rose is reported to have wept at the news and pined away.

By 1875 Rose was diagnosed as suffering from an unsound mind (she had frequent epileptic fits), and it was decided that she should be consigned to a lunatic asylum in Gloucester. On the day she was due to go, 17 November 1875, a fresh tragedy occurred. A maid found Rose suffocated in her bed after Mr Carrington had left for London. On her doctor's instructions Rose had been taking chloral, an unrestricted anaesthetic medication which was routinely administered by her husband in Hungarian wine. On the morning of Rose's death, Mr Carrington had got up and got dressed. He had not tried speaking with his wife (although they shared a double bed) and, oddly, hadn't noticed that she was dead.

Jumps House with wings added, around 1940

Suspicions abounded. Bruising was found on Rose's arms, but an inquest held at the Devil's Jumps Inn on 21 November deemed this bruising to be unassociated with her death. The coroner ruled that "any domestic disagreement or even blows that might have been struck, if not affecting the cause of death, was outside the enquiry". An open verdict was declared, and Richard Carrington was heavily censured for his neglect. Carrington immediately left home for a week. He was seen re-entering the house on 27 November, only to find that all the servants had deserted. He was not to be seen alive again.

The astronomer's body was soon found, mysteriously, in a servant's small room, locked from the inside. Carrington had a tea-leaf poultice over one ear, probably indicating acute earache or toothache. He, too, had taken chloral. Again, an inquest was held at the Devil's Jumps Inn, and it was determined that he had probably died of a 'the rupture of a blood vessel on the brain'. Officially, the verdict was that Carrington died of natural causes. The life of an eminent astronomer – speculated by some to be the next Astronomer Royal – had ended tragically, prematurely, mysteriously and controversially.

One final twist: Carrington's will, dated 9 January 1873, declared that "I desire that if I die in England, I may be buried at a depth of between 10 and 12 feet in the ground surrounding my freehold house at Churt aforesaid at an expense not exceeding five pounds and without any service being read over my grave or any memorial being erected to my memory and that after my death neither my chin be shaved nor my shirt changed".

So where is the body? Research by well-known Churt resident Melene Barnes, who lived in Jumps House for many years, showed that, contrary to his wishes and contrary to reports, Carrington appears to be buried in the family mausoleum in West Norwood, as is his wife Rose. At least his name is engraved there.

Carrington's and Rose's ghosts were believed to haunt Jumps House. In the 1890s parts of the building were demolished by the then owner Lord Ashcombe, allegedly to drive away the ghosts. A habitable core of three rooms was left to be occupied by his gamekeeper, Albert Criddle.

In the 1920s Frank Mason, a well-known Churt benefactor, bought Jumps House and built the adjacent Borrow House. The latter was a wedding present for his daughter, Molly, on her marriage to ex-First World War naval hero Commander Vincent Cottrell.

As a gunnery officer of RMSP *Demerara*, Cottrell is credited with sinking the first German U-boat of the war. He expanded Jumps House, adding 'girls' wings' to achieve the unusual colonial-style hybrid that we have today.

Vincent Cottrell as Chief Officer after the
Great War

Any sign of ghosts is long gone. Today, the house is peaceful and the wooded surrounds are a haven for deer, badgers, foxes and rabbits. There is a recently discovered silted-up well; however, I wonder what lies at the bottom beneath all that silt!

William Tate, August 2004

Bibliography

Richard Carrington, *A Catalogue of 3735 Circumpolar Stars, 1857*
Richard Carrington, *Observations on the Spots on the Sun*, 1863
Agnes M. Clerke, *A Popular History of Astronomy During the Nineteenth Century*, reprinted 2003
Olivia Cotton, *Churt - An Oasis Through Time*, 1998
Dictionary of National Biography, 'Carrington, Richard Christopher'
J. Alfred Eggar, *Life and Customs in Gilbert White's, Cobbett's and Charles Kingsley's Country*, London: Simpkin, Marshall, Hamilton, Kent & Co. Ltd., 1929
Norman C. Keer, *The Life and Times of Richard Christopher Carrington*, 1996
Journal of The British Astronomical Association, Vol. 83, No. 2, 1973
Monthly Notices of The Royal Astronomical Society, Vol. xxx, 10 December 1869 ; and Carrington's obituary, Vol. 36, p. 137, 1875-6
Rex Morgan, *A Glimpse of Frank Mason's Churt*, The Runciman Press, 1988
Derek Walker-Smith and Edward Clarke [Defending Barrister], *The Life of Sir Edward Clarke*, London: Butterworth, 1939
NEWSPAPERS
Farnham and Haslemere Herald, [letter by R. D. Clarke], November 1949
Hampshire Chronicle, 26 August 1871, p.7, col. 2
Hampshire Chronicle, 2 September 1871, p.8, col. 3
Hampshire Chronicle, 9 September, 1871, p.8, col. 2
Surrey and Hampshire News, ('Drama on Devil's Jumps'), 21 December 1922, p. 6, col. 3 & 4
Surrey and Hampshire News, (letter), 11 September 1947
The Surrey Advertiser, 26 August 1871
The Surrey Advertiser, 20 November 1875, p. 8, col. 1
The Surrey Advertiser, 27 November 1875, p. 2, col. 3
The Surrey Advertiser, 04 December 1875, p. 4, col. 3
The Surrey Advertiser, 11 December 1875, p. 2, col. 4
The Times, 22 November 1875, p. 5, col. 3
The Times, 3 December 1875, p. 10, col. 2
The Times, 7 December 1875, p. 11, col. 6

15: Over the Years in Photographs

Local Inns

The Crossways Inn

Crossways Inn in the 1890s

Brooks described the old inn as a typical 3- or 4-bay 16th Century house. This was the building which the School Managers objected to when they started to build the school in 1871. They asked the magistrates to refuse a further licence but were unsuccessful in their request.

As owned by Farnham Breweries c. 1894

(From account book) Statement from Farnham United Breweries regarding their purchase of the Crossways Inn in September 1895 for £1,000. Rebuilding and improvements resulted in a value of £1,630 14s 10d by the following September, 1896

Courage Beers bought the inn in 1927

Crossways Inn, c. 1910

Crossways Inn in the 1980s

The Pride of the Valley, built in 1870

Believed to be about 1880

Probably about late 1920

The White Horse Inn or Frensham Pond Hotel

The Pond Hotel is approached from Two Counties Lane - Surrey and Hampshire

T E Lawrence is said to have taken refuge here from the media in 1923.
He certainly visited Lloyd George in Churt.

The garden, Frensham Pond Hotel

Telegrams: "Mercer, Frensham Pond, Churt."
Telephone No. 121, Farnham.

FRENSHAM POND HOTEL,
NR. FARNHAM, SURREY

View of the pond and hotel as it appeared in their advertising brochure.

A further view of Two Counties Lane

The road in 2003

The Mariners

Two views of The Mariners.

Views of the Garage

Older residents remember when the garage consisted of one petrol pump outside a corrugated iron building. It was run by Percy Kinge, who was in charge when Ruth Deadman was a girl.

The house to its left was first a butcher's run by Nick Marshall, then a tuckshop in the hands of Miss Charman

Mr Mason is believed to have owned the land on which a new garage was built. It was run by Kinge then "Tug" Charman.

At that time Mrs Grimes, Sr, was living at Grayshott where she had a garage. She also had a 14-seater charabanc which took schoolchildren from Churt to Shottermill for woodwork lessons.

Churt Garage over the years

Moreton Close under construction. Note the Bus Stop

The garage after rebuilding

The garage in 2004

Churt's Celebration of King George V's Silver Jubilee in 1935

Scouts outside their hut opposite the Village Hall

Note the original pavilion

Schooldays at Churt

An early school group
of unknown date

Mr Rankine, with the senior
boys, in his schoolhouse
garden about 1907.

Standards V and VI in 1906
with Mr Rankine

Eric Larby is at the extreme left of this 1908 school photograph. His sister Ruth wears a bow and is 5th of the girls standing. Another sister Agnes is also in the group.

St. John's School, Churt.

REPORT on Scholar's Work, Term ending......*Christmas*............1909

Name......*Eric Larby*........................ Standard *V.*

Attendance *9a.* Punctuality *9a.*

Eric's progress during the present year has been excellent; he is painstaking and very intelligent. He is a great credit to us. WFR

ARITHMETIC {Mental {Written	9 / 9	NEEDLEWORK	...	...	
READING	9	NATURE STUDY	9
WRITING	8	RECITATION	9
SPELLING	7	HISTORY	
COMPOSITION	9	GEOGRAPHY	9 ? 00
DRAWING (a) Freehand (b) Brushwork	7	*Current* GARDENING	10
			96

Possible Marks in each subject : 10.

Class Teacher......*W. F. Rankine*

Head Master : W. F. RANKINE.

A term report of 1909 when Mr Rankine was headmaster.

Schooldays at Churt

This is one of three remarkable papers that are the roll call of pupils attending St John's School when the annual inspection by His Majesty's Inspectors took place on 4th June 1875, three years after the school opened.

77

Names of the Children presented to the Inspector

11 a.m. (H.M. 21 on June 4th 1875.

No.	Name	R	W	a	No. attend.	Age mths.	date adm.	Class
1	Henry Chuter	x	x	o	252	9	-	-	-
2	James Wheeler	x	x	o	288	9	73	4	3
3	Stephen Aldred	o	o	o	323	9	74	7
4	Rose Matthews	x	x	x	386	7	72	2
5	Sarah Ann Martin	x	x	x	378	7
6	Minnie Croucher	x	x	x	361	7	73	4
7	Alice Glaisher	x	x	x	344	7	72	3
8	Alice Shrubb	x	x	x	383	7
9	Ellen Glaisher	x	x	x	358	7	74	1
10	Edwin Holden	o	o	x	366	9	72	5	2	1	2
11	Frank Baker	x	x	o	371	8
12	William Croy	x	x	o	299	9
13	George Shrubb	x	x	o	379	9	73	3
14	George Fullick	o	o	x	299	10	72
15	George Mauley	x	x	x	283	11	4
16	William Tilbury	o	x	o	371	12	1
17	James Aslett	x	x	x	308	9	74	5
18	Louisa Holden	x	x	x	292	12	4
19	Bertha Marshall	x	x	x	281	10
20	Flora Marshall	o	o	o	360	8
21	Mary J. Holden	x	x	x	352	9	5

127

The columns of the roll call list:
  pupil's name
  results in reading, writing and arithmetic
  number of attendances over the school year, morning and afternoon
  counting as two
  age last birthday
  date of admission
  class
  last Standard
  present Standard

The outcome of this inspection was available in July 1875:

"The discipline is good and the school has improved in respect of instruction. The reading of the younger children is very indistinct and in the 2nd Standard the children's knowledge of notation is confused and unsatisfactory, and their spelling re-quires attention. The work of the elder children is done with very fair neatness and ac-curacy.

Miss Must will shortly receive her certificate."

Research by Peter Larby has disclosed the addresses of most of the pupils list-ed. Peter, a pupil at Churt school, later graduated and taught at Farnham Grammar School.

Picture of the Larby family.
The boy in the sailor suit, Eric Larby, became father of our
researcher Peter. Two sons at the right were to die in World War I.

Headmaster Charles Tubb, appointed in September 1925, is seen with staff.
Mrs Sanders is seated centre. He stayed until 1937, a period when there were
a number of significant changes to the educational system.
In 1931 teachers' salaries were reduced by 10% under the National Economy Act.

School photo of Standard 1 in 1925 with Mrs Sanders, teacher.

School photo of Standard 3 in 1925.

School photo of Standard 4 in 1925.

Several pictures taken during Charles Tubb's headship. His son Monty is
at the right front in the above group.

More pictures taken during Charles Tubb's headship.

21st Century Pupils

All the pupils took part in The Sleepy Shepherd in December 2003

Part of the cast in the 2003 Christmas production of "A Present for the Baby": Amy Wilkinson, George Smale, Pippa Herring, Jack Dawes, Vicky Winston, Grace Casely and Millie Rawlinson.

July 2004. St John's School gave a surprise tea party for
Mrs Ronagh Wheeler on her retirement from teaching.

Places, People and Events

Places

The Tuckshop 1946

Churt Crossways 1954

Gravel Hill, The Bourne, coming towards Churt, about 1910

The Bourne 1910; coming from Churt

Silverbeck Lodge about 1944

Barford Pond

Barford Pond

Views of Whitmore Valley

The Churt Valley around Whitmore

Whitmore Valley

The house on the Jump, formerly Hook's Skyparlour, 1949

140

People

J A Allardyce who gave devoted service to Rushmoor Church

Tom Martin of Churt's Old Post Office when the area was known as "St. Martin's Square"

Michael Stenning (right) Churt's postmaster until his retirement in 2004, talks with Norman Lingard at a school Open Day

April 2003 Churt became a Parish Council. Standing outside the village hall are the new councillors: Chris Hicks, Derek Sibley, Peter Cotton, Shirley Lingard, Christine Pointer Head of Waverley District Council, Murray Reece, Tim Kilpatrick and Tom Viveash, with Bryn Morgan, Clerk to the Council. John Petty and Mike Jordan were not present.

Events

Churt cricket team at Thursley 1927

1949 A group of winners of games trophies presented by Mr A Caro
at Churt Working Men's Club. Seated (L to R) Messrs G Wonham, R Silvester,
A Caro, A Mitchell, H Woods, W A C Voller. Standing: Messrs P Pelling,
E Farminer, J C Mitchell, H Marshall, S Martin

May 1987 Mrs Ethel White (centre) at St John's Church, Churt, where she served as cleaner for 38 years, found friends had arranged a retirement surprise at the church on Saturday, 16th May 1987 Back row: Audrey Mitchell, Peter Slater, Penelope Barnsdale, Peter Gunter, Tony Barnsdale, Tony Duncan In front: Molly Slater, Janet Gunter, Grace Flemming, Pam Eames

1987 The Rev George Parkinson declares officially open the new church youth building at Churt, to be known as The Stables

1991 Churt Fete on the recreation ground:
Audrey Beevers, Sally Fraser, David Jeffreson, Guy Bach, Jane Jeffreson,
Anne Taylor, Arthur Taylor

2003 The WI presents a flag pole to Churt to commemorate the Queen's Golden Jubilee. Brian Thomas hoists the Union Jack.

2004 Residents undertake the first Beating the Bounds under the new Parish Council.
Participants include Peter Cotton, Sandy Watson, Ann Richmond, Richard Norton,
Elizabeth Norton, Sylvia Sibley, Maureen Butler, John Richmond, Carol Elam, Millie Bryant,
Chris Hicks, June Christie, David Hillberry, Sondra Hillberry, Tim Kilpatrick, John Christie,
Eileen Kilpatrick, Shirley Song and Derek Sibley

Michael Stenning, Churt's popular postmaster, raises his glass
at a retirement party given in his honour. 2004

Churt Amateur Dramatic Society

1980 - 2005

CADS

Silver Anniversary

CADS' first production, "White Sheep of the Family", was performed in 1980. Taking a photo call are: Back L to R : Sandra Graham, Michael Stenning, Geoff Gage, Mike Pennick, John Ferris, Stuart Croucher Seated: Alex Lingard, Liz Barker, Carol Madgwick

Wardrobe Mistress 1980. Elsie Burchmore with some of her costumes

2002: 'Allo 'Allo Standing L-R: John Millais, Michael Condé, Caroline Lusher, Duncan Carmichael-Jack, David Searle, David Forster, Nigel Wadham, Peter Christopherson, Andrew Meehan, Tracey St John Taylor, Wanda Irwin Seated L-R: Dawn Barrow, Anneliese Wadham, James Woodley, Vivienne Raeside, Sandy Seagrove

Acknowledgements

I acknowledge with gratitude the help given by fellow residents of Churt who have willingly answered my questions and helped in so many ways.

I would also like to thank:

Joan Aldrich
John Burrill
Thomas Carter
Tim Childerhouse
Edward Croucher
Colin Dodds
Dan Finnigan
Patricia Honychurch
Bill Houghton
Peter Larby
Frank Martin

George Miskin
Michael & Josette Napier
Jackie Pentacost
Sir Richard Posnett
Len Rapley
J O Smith
Monty Tubb
Marguerite Wills
Surrey Local History Centre, Woking
The Rural Life Museum, Tilford
The Museum of Farnham

Index